# CASTLE COMMANDO

## Donald Gilchrist

PUBLISHED BY
WEST HIGHLAND MUSEUM PUBLISHING

# Author's note to the 'Colonel'

My Dear Charles,

Here is your book about wartime Achnacarry.

It is not my intention in it, or elsewhere, to claim any particular glory for Commandos. The Battle Honours of regiments speak for themselves. Nor do I uphold one nation. The Combined Operations' motto is 'United we Conquer'. I believe you would have it so. Rather do I seek to remind myself and others of the legendary nature of the Colonel and his Castle in the North.

I have to thank the many friends who have contributed to the task given to me. In particular I wish to thank Bill Gilmour Smith and Colin Neil MacKay for their generous help and guidance.

But it is to you, Charles, that we who counted it an honour to serve you, wish to show our appreciation. You made us fit to fight. You taught us the art of living in a world at war, and to laugh in the most perilous circumstances. What we were – if we were anything – we owe in great measure to you.

Donald

1960

# ACKNOWLEDGEMENTS

Thanks are due to the Commando Association, appointed Freemen of Lochaber by Lochaber District Council, who supported the idea of a reprint of this book. Especial thanks are due to Major James Dunning, founder member of No 4 Commando (1940) and Commando instructor at Achnacarry 1943 – 1945, who wrote the appreciation of Donald Gilchrist and supplied the text from which the section on the Commando Trail was taken.

Photographs were provided by Alex Gillespie, Fort William, Rob Fairley, Lochailort, the Clan Cameron Museum, Achnacarry, the Commando Museum, Spean Bridge Hotel and the West Highland Museum, Fort William. Mrs Rosemary Anne Gilchrist very kindly supplied a photograph of her late husband. Grateful thanks are here recorded to the Lochaber Area Committee of the Highland Council for financial assistance towards the reprinting of this book.

West Highland Museum,
Fort William, 2005

ISBN 0-9502579-1-5 / 978-0-9502579-1-4

First published 1960

Reprinted 1960 by Oliver & Boyd Ltd

Reprinted 1993 for Lochaber District Council

Reprinted for West Highland Museum
by Highland Printers Ltd, Inverness 2005

*Donald Gilchrist 1914-2001*

This Book is dedicated
to the young Boy
Gillian
and
to the little Girl
Sally-Anne
so that they may recognise
The Three Men on the Hill
at Spean Bridge
in Lochaber

# FOREWORD

BY

ADMIRAL OF THE FLEET

## THE EARL MOUNTBATTEN OF BURMA

K.G.  P.C.  C.G.B.  G.C.S.I.  G.C.I.E  G.C.V.O.  D.S.O.

BEFORE a new technique in fighting, which involves a special form of courage and self-sacrifice, can be successfully exploited, three stages are essential. Firstly the whole idea has to be thought up and thought out. Secondly the right type of volunteers have to be obtained, and thirdly highly specialised training must be arranged. This book deals with the third phase, training.

The right site had to be found, and the right man. Achnacarry could hardly have been bettered for the site, and Charles Vaughan could certainly not have been bettered as the man.

So successful was the Commando Training that, under various names, such as Battle Schools and Ranger Training, something approaching this technique was adopted by most of the allied forces.

I shall never forget the impact Achnacarry made on me when I visited it in 1942, after taking over the Combined Operations Command, and I suspect that neither will those who went through the course, since many told me later that they found the real thing less alarming than the 'Opposed Landing Exercise' with which Charles Vaughan used to finish up each course.

1960

Mountbatten of Burma
A.F.

# DONALD GILCHRIST

In 1960, some fifteen years after the Second World War, Donald Gilchrist fulfilled a wartime promise to write a book about the famous Commando Training centre based at the historic castle of Achnacarry. Donald was well qualified to write this account, for not only had he undergone his initial Commando training there after volunteering for this Special Service Force, but he had subsequently seen active service in Lord Lovat's No 4 Commando on the fateful Dieppe Raid in August 1942.

But that's not all; after the Raid, Donald was promoted to a Troop Leader and then made adjutant of No 4, a unique British unit with two French Commando Troops, and earmarked to play a leading part in the liberation of North West Europe starting with the storming of the beaches of Normandy on D Day 1944.

For some eighty-three days Donald was involved with the Commando in the battle to hold the bridgehead over the river Orne on the Allies' eastern flank, and in the subsequent break-out. It was for his distinguished service during this prolonged campaign that Donald was awarded the Croix de Guerre.

Shortly afterwards Donald was posted to Achnacarry as Colonel Vaughan's adjutant and it was during this tour of duty that he made the promise to write this book. Following the end of hostilities whilst No 4 was involved with the duties of the occupation of Germany, Donald returned to the unit as the second-in-command, and was ultimately demobilised and returned to his peacetime employment with the Royal Bank of Scotland but not before his marriage to Rosemary Anne. They had met whilst she was serving with the Women's Auxiliary Service (ATS).

So ended a distinguished wartime service which had, in fact, started before the War, when Donald joined the Territorial Army in 1938 and was commissioned in the Cameronians (Scottish Rifles). This was later recognised with the award of the Territorial Decoration (TD).

Born in 1914 in Paisley he attended the local Grammar School and the Barbour Academy, then went into banking with the Royal Bank of Scotland. He spent all his working years with them for he returned to the Renfrew branch on demobilisation from the army in 1945 and subsequently managed the Ayr branch. In that town he was prominent in various community activities, and for many years was the Ayr Chamber of Commerce representative on the West of Scotland War Pensions Committee. A keen golfer he was a member of the Royal Troon Golf Club.

He was also a talented painter in oils and he enjoyed writing, for in addition to this title he later wrote a sequel, 'DON'T CRY FOR ME' (the Commandos – D Day and After)' which was published in 1982.

However, one of his greatest moments came in 1975 when he was invited by his French Commando comrades to participate in a large official parade to commemorate the deeds and valour of those Frenchmen and close allies who had fought in the battle of liberation, and he was honoured to carry out the ceremony of lighting the flame at the Arc de Triomphe in the presence of the French President. M. Mitterand.

Rosemary and Donald had two children, a son Gill and a daughter Sally-Anne, and later they were blessed with four grandchildren. At the age of 87 Donald died in 2001, but this book is a splendid testimony to a gallant wartime Commando soldier and a fitting tribute to the thousands of Commandos who underwent their rigorous wartime training at Achnacarry – 'Castle Commando'.

James Dunning
Founder member of No 4 Commando (1940) and
Commando Instructor Achnacarry 1943 – 1945

# 1

I AWOKE to the steady, undramatic throbbing of the ship's engines. As I shaved, washed and dressed with my usual care, I told myself if the worst came to the worst I would at least make a well-groomed corpse. Then I went to breakfast. It was all rather disappointingly routine and normal to someone going on his first raid, as I was. A Hollywood director would have yelled 'Cut!' and made us do it all again.

The Mess Decks gave the impression that there was a Hallowe'en party in the offing – and not a Commando operation. Everywhere men were applying grease-paint to their faces. It varied in depth of colour. Some had achieved the desired nigger minstrel effect. Others looked more like Red Indians.

A Sioux Brave in khaki approached me. 'You haven't got your face blackened yet, sir. I'll fix it for you.'

He smeared my face with a brown, greasy substance, the smell of which almost made me sick.

'Where the hell did you get that?' I demanded.

'Right from the cook's pan, sir,' he grinned.

The ship's engines slowed. Every light was dowsed. There came a shrill blast on the bo'sun's pipe. Our signal to embark on the assault landing craft.

It was just before dawn. Slowly, in single file, we went up the companion-ways into the cold darkness of the upper deck, and into the small craft hanging on the davits. With a rustle of well-oiled chains, the L.C.A.s were lowered into the sea. A brief exchange of profane pleasantries with any naval ratings about.

Then the engines whirred and we were off.

Next to me was a veteran Commando, Gunner Smith. He wore spectacles with metal rims. A tommy-gun was cradled lovingly in his arms. Across the muzzle was a strip of adhesive tape to prevent water getting in when he splashed ashore. Gunner Herd, my runner, was on my other side.

The minutes quickly passed in whispers.

'There's the lighthouse.'

The speaker was the leader of B Troop, Captain Gordon Webb. The lighthouse was our landmark. Its grey, pencil shape could just be made out in the half light. We were all on our feet in the boat. There was an excited buzz of conversation.

'Shut up, and get down,' Webb rapped out.

The L.C.A. was at half speed now, silently slipping towards the shore as a grey band of light crept across the horizon. Tense now, we wondered – was it going to be a dry landing? Was it going to be unopposed?

It wasn't.

A stream of tracer bullets suddenly leapt out at us from behind the beach, searching, probing. A mortar thumped as the L.C.A. grated on the shingle. Webb cursed and clutched his shoulder where he had been hit by a mortar fragment. The ramp clattered down, and we swept up the beach, Webb still with us. On either side of us, all along the beach, other L.C.A.s were grounding, other ramps going down, other Commandos were racing ashore.

We were in occupied France. This was the Dieppe raid. Our particular objective was a German gun battery at Varengeville. I was in action for the first time. A keen young junior officer. Proud to be a Section Leader in No. 4 Commando. Determined to be a credit to my country and an inspiration to my men. And then…

Then my trousers started coming down!

I still shudder whenever I think of it. Between curses, I blamed equally German barbed wire and the British battle-dress buttons – both made of metal, and both notoriously sharp.

My Section was one of the first over that barbed wire, right on the heels of Sergeant Watkins and his reconnaissance party. We were advancing in the face of fairly heavy mortar and machine-gun fire. Under such circumstances the first men over a barbed wire entanglement are expected to trample on it, wrench at it, and roll about on it to flatten a passage for those following behind.

In my enthusiasm I did everything a rogue elephant would have done except trumpet. As if in protest against these unnatural strains and stresses, British buttons showed their metal and sawed themselves free from my battledress.

And down slid my trousers.

It was a moment of mental anguish. Dieppe was no place for a man to be caught with his pants down. No. 4 Commando was firing at the Germans. And the Germans, notoriously lacking in a sense of humour, were firing back. What a ludicrous target I would present! In addition to the long list of charges he had already levelled against British troops, Lord Haw-Haw would now be able to put 'indecent exposure'.

Clutching my trousers in one hand, tommy-gun in the other, I raced inland. But those abominable battledress buttons had reduced my morale to rock bottom. If any of my comrades had noticed my predicament, and had said one wrong word – I'd probably have shot him dead and then burst into tears.

Happily for me, the hour produced the man – in the shape of a poker-faced Commando private. And the man produced the very words needed to give me back my confidence.

This providential private and I ran shoulder to shoulder for some seconds. An almost solid stream of German machine-gun tracer bullets was whizzing past at about head height. We were forced to run like half-shut knives, our bodies bent forward, as if we were forcing our way against a strong wind.

The private took a couple of quick glances – one up at the arc of enemy fire, the other across at me. Then, out of the side of his mouth, he panted: 'Jesus Christ, sir, this is nearly as bad as Achnacarry!'

If I'd had time I'd have stopped and laughed my head off. As it was I went tearing on, grinning all over my face.

In German-occupied France an English soldier had thought of a remote part of the Highlands of Scotland. And he'd been so right. At Achnacarry we'd spent half our time shambling along like Charles Laughton as 'The Hunchback of Notre Dame' under a hail of live ammunition.

This *was* nearly as bad as Achnacarry.

With an almost contemptuous wrench and twist, I made my trousers more or less secure around my waist. I was dressed, if not quite properly dressed. To hell with all trousers – I was in the war again.

A moment later word was passed along to halt, to allow closing up. No sooner had we done so than the tall, debonair figure of No. 4 Commando's C.O., Lord Lovat, appeared. He was informally attired in corduroy slacks and a grey sweater with 'Lovat' sewn across it. A

Winchester sporting rifle hung rakishly from the crook of his arm. He looked as if he was out for a pleasant day's shooting on the moors.

Giving us a reproachful glance he demanded, 'Why isn't someone up with the recce group giving them some encouragement?'

It was nearly as bad as Achnacarry, all right. At Achnacarry, too, we were frequently expected to be in two places at once.

Military experts have described the part played by No. 4 Commando in the Dieppe raid as one of the most successful Commando operations of the war. Since I was on it, I'd be the last one to argue the point. On the other hand, who am I to justify the statement?

That would require a neatly rounded, overall picture – which isn't the way I remember the destruction of the gun battery at Varengeville at all. Despite the impression given by authors of many war books – both fiction and non-fiction – it just isn't possible for a man taking part in a battle to be everywhere, see everything, and remember it all. He only remembers the incidents he himself took part in – and not even all of those. Often it is the most trivial incidents that remain in the mind, such as the descent of my trousers.

One of my most vivid memories is of the first German I ever saw killed. Boston Havocs were screaming over and around the enemy position, marking it for us. Like an ungainly, grey-uniformed grouse, a German broke cover and ran across a field. He wasn't fast enough. One of the Havocs swooped. A burst of cannon fire hit him and lifted him off his feet, hurling him for several yards before he tumbled head over heels and lay still.

Through a thick hedge we could see an anti-aircraft tower overlooking the battery position. A few Germans were moving about on top of it. The Bostons were buzzing about like hornets.

The troop had now closed up and we crawled round to the rear of the position. It seemed as if the Germans were unaware they had visitors entering by the back door.

Gordon Webb gave the order to fire. Rifles cracked. We watched amazed as a German soldier on top of the tower toppled over the edge and slowly fell to the ground some eighty feet below – like an Indian from a cliff in a Western picture.

Delighted at his success, the marksman turned to Gordon and said, 'Now do I get my bloody proficiency pay, sir?'

I recognised the man. A few weeks before he'd had his pay reduced by a sixpence for a bad score on the range.

Webb said, 'I want a few of you to go round and knock out the right-hand gun.' He looked at me. I got up to find Sergeant Watkins and a few others already on their feet, Marshall, Keeley and Hurd.

We cut across a hedge, raced through some trees, and darted between two buildings. Before us, not seventy-five yards away, was the battery position, German heads bobbing up and down. We began to stalk – we'd learned how at Achnacarry – walking upright, stiff-legged, our weapons at the ready. Suddenly, we froze.

A German soldier had appeared from a hedge which ran parallel to and behind the battery. He was carrying a box of grenades. He must have sensed danger. He stopped, turned cautiously, and looked open-mouthed at us. Horror distorted his face. Then, still holding the box of grenades in both hands in front of him, he started to jump up and down like a baby in a temper while he shouted dementedly, 'Kommando, Kommando!'

A sarcastic voice at my side said, 'I'll give him flippin' Commando!' A rifle spat its bullet, and the German fell dead over his grenades.

Close to us the hedge rustled. The Bren leapt in Marshall's hands. I glanced in surprise at a grey form now huddled in a heap. Up went a hand grenade to explode in the right-hand gun pit. Groans were coupled with a Cockney voice: 'Every time a coconut!'

We were ready to go in.

With fixed bayonets D Troop attacked from the right, yelling like banshees. In too came my own B Troop, led by Gordon Webb. His right hand was dangling, useless – but he had a revolver in his left. Razor-sharp, burnished Sheffield steel tore the guts out of the Varengeville battery. Screams, smoke, the smell of burning cordite. Mad moments soon over.

A rifle shot from the buildings behind the hedge made us steal up to peer through. Lying in a yard was a wounded Commando soldier. From the gloom of a barn emerged the German soldier who had cut him down. He jumped up and crashed his boots down on the face of the wounded Commando.

Our weapons came up instantaneously. A corporal in our group raised his hand. Automatically, we held our fire. The corporal took careful aim and squeezed the trigger. The German clutched the pit of his stomach as if trying to claw the bullet out. He tried to scream, but couldn't. Slowly, he crumpled to the ground to twist and turn in agony. I looked at my companions. Four pairs of eyes in faces blackened for action stared coldly at his suffering. They were eyes of stone. No gloating, no pity. Just honest hate for an enemy who knew no code and had no compassion.

We doubled across the yard to where the two wounded lay side by side. For our comrade – morphine. For the beast – a bayonet thrust.

At the guns, Jimmy MacKay, the other Section Leader in B Troop, was fitting special explosive charges into the breech of each gun. In a satisfied tone he was saying: 'Fit just like a glove – just like a glove.' I wondered what he would have said if these heavy charges which he had carried from early morning had not fitted.

Lovat's next words brought me to my feet.

'Set them on fire,' he ordered, with a gesture at the surrounding buildings. 'Burn the lot.'

These were not the words of a commanding officer in the British Army. They were the words of a Highland chief bent on the total destruction of the enemy.

As we withdrew to the beach a black pall of smoke covered the corpse of the German gun battery at Varengeville.

On the shore Lovat yelled at the Navy to come a bit closer. 'No reason why I should get my feet wet,' he said.

Aboard the landing craft, heading out from the beach, some of F Troop were eating apples. While attacking enemy positions through an orchard, they had found time to fill their pockets. An escapade in the best schoolboy tradition – if you substitute enemy bullets for the curses of an irate orchard owner.

Aircraft were dodging and winging about overhead. A Bren gunner had a shot at one marked with a swastika, using his pal as a mounting by getting him to hold the legs of the gun above his head.

We watched a dog fight between two planes – one German, the other American. Smoke belched from the American plane, and its pilot baled out. He fluttered down and drifted towards our L.C.A. which changed course to go to his rescue.

It was a fantastic piece of work. The Yank pilot hit the sea alongside our boat, and was hauled aboard by his parachute almost simultaneously. The Commandos sat him down. Somebody stuck a tin of self-heating soup into his hand. The American gazed at it dazedly, incredulously. A voice enquired, 'How's that for service, bud?'

We were told that we were now in reserve, and might have to go in again at Dieppe itself. But shortly after we had transferred the wounded to a hospital ship, orders were given to return to England in the L.C.A.s.

Soon we could see the white cliffs. We were home. Our part in the Dieppe raid was over.

On the quayside there were Intelligence Officers, photographers, newspaper men, and a Canadian Reception Post. The Canadians gave us Sweet Caporal cigarettes, matches, mugs of tea. We were allowed to send a short telegram home. We could mention Dieppe. Faced with this uncensored opportunity, we were at a loss for words.

To our questions we were given answers.

The other Commando in the raid, No. 3, whose task was similar to ours, but north of Dieppe, had run into trouble at sea. They had been broken up. But a handful under Peter Young and Ruxton had managed to swim ashore. With their rifles they had sniped at the German gun battery to such effect that the Germans had lowered the sights of their huge guns to 'snipe' back. This peculiar battle went on all day and prevented the German guns from firing on the main landing at Dieppe.

And although the Canadians had taken a mauling, they had done plenty of mauling themselves.

It had been a day of heroic deeds. I had been surrounded by them. But one in particular stood out in my mind.

Some of No. 4 Commando had been wounded on landing. Too seriously wounded to be moved. As we went on to the German gun battery a medical orderly called Pasquali had waited behind to attend to them. The beach from which we withdrew was some distance away. Pasquali was fit. He was unwounded. He could easily have walked along the shore and returned with us to England.

Instead, he chose to stay with the wounded...

That was Dieppe.

What with one thing and another, it had – as that private had succinctly put it – been nearly as bad as Achnacarry.

# 2

ACHNACARRY was the place of which 25,000 or so Commandos once said – on being posted there – 'Where the bloody hell is that?'

It was in the heart of the Scottish Highlands, Inverness-shire, near... Well, it wasn't really near anywhere. The nearest railway station was at Spean Bridge, eight miles away. And it was even further to the nearest town of any size, Fort William.

A God-forsaken spot? To many, possibly, yes. But God help anyone who says so if there should happen to be a man called Cameron within earshot!

Achnacarry is the spiritual headquarters of the Clan Cameron. The land belongs to the Camerons. A land of proud Cameron tradition. And in the centre of it all stands a picturesque, centuries-old castle known as Achnacarry House – home of the hereditary chief of the clan, Cameron of Lochiel.

It was at Achnacarry House, between the years of 1942 and 1945, that a new expression was given to the English language. An expression that is widely used today, and will probably still be used for decades to come. An expression containing just two words: 'Commando training.'

During those three years, Cameron of Lochiel went into voluntary exile. Achnacarry House was taken over by the military authorities. Nissen huts sprang up in the castle grounds. The Cameron tartan gave way to khaki. The Cameron hills echoed to English, Welsh, Irish, French, Belgian, American, Dutch, Norwegian cries, commands, and curses. Achnacarry House became in turn the Commando Depot, and later the Commando Basic Training Centre.

Here, in the heart of the Scottish Highlands, fighting men from nearly every land underwent a period of training designed to stretch human stamina to the utmost. Here, after weeks in which they marvelled at how much their own bodies could stand, they finally qualified for the honour of wearing green berets. They became Commandos.

In short, it was at Achnacarry that the men were separated from the boys... The men were posted to the various Commandos. The boys who couldn't last the pace were returned to their original unit.

You will meet ex-Commandos who will stoutly deny ever having seen Achnacarry. Prior to 1942, the system was more or less to put the cart before the horse. Volunteers were formed into Commando groups and then given their training. This process worked well enough at the time, and in most cases, produced an excellent type of fighting man.

But the day came when the demand for Commandos exceeded the supply. A day when Commandos had to be mass-produced. And the assembly line started at Achnacarry. Here the raw material was to be forged into soldiers who required only a little polishing before they were fit for the landing craft, the beaches, and the enemy garrisons.

The raw material was there – no lack of volunteers from ordinary Army units. And Achnacarry was there. All that was required was an organising genius; someone who could work the spell that transforms an ordinary soldier into a super-fit, super-confident, resourceful Commando. Was there a man in all the ranks of the Army brass-hats who could make a success of such a task? The powers-that-be in Whitehall have acquired a reputation for trying to fit square pegs into round holes. Yet I have a sneaking feeling that somewhere – right up at the top level – is someone who knows what he's doing.

For the round hole of Achnacarry, they chose a man who appeared to be the squarest peg imaginable. They chose Lieutenant-Colonel Charles Edward Vaughan.

At first glance, Vaughan seemed the most unsuitable man in the world to produce an entirely new type of soldier – a soldier encouraged to think for himself.

Vaughan was 'Army' to his back teeth. He had risen from the ranks, having been at one time a Regimental Sergeant-Major in the Guards. He was a Londoner by birth. His voice was unique. It could be soft, even fatherly, but changed to the sudden blast of the Guards R.S.M. – all leapt galvanised into statuesque attention, and even inspecting Generals guiltily squared their shoulders, and thumbed the seams of their trousers. He had a habit, when roused, of running his words together, and occasionally dropping an 'aitch'. Like most Englishmen he could not pronounce 'Loch' but spoke of it as 'Lock'. There were times when he did not understand my language. At no time did anyone misunderstand his. All hastened to satisfy his requests. All leapt to obey his commands.

It was on a bleak February day in 1942 that Vaughan travelled North in a staff car to take up his new duties. He was a tall man, heavily built, with an expansive, jowled face, and a determined jutting jaw. As his car went quickly through the countryside just outside Fort William on the last stages of his journey, Vaughan sat in a corner of the back seat, deep in thought.

His mind went back to the interview with the Brigadier of Special Service Brigade, Charles Hayden, that had led to his new duties. 'Charles, we shall have to look forward,' Hayden had said. 'Sooner or later Special Service Brigade will be called on to lead the assault. We must have the men and the reserves. We must have the right sort of men. Tough, self-reliant chaps with bags of initiative. Men with guts, fit to fight. Men with the will to win.'

Vaughan glanced out of the window at the rugged Scottish landscape and stirred uncomfortably in his seat. He was an Englishman, a Londoner. How would he get on with the Scots who lived in these parts? He had heard about the Highlanders. A wild, clannish lot with a historical bias against English soldiers.

As the stern shape of Ben Nevis loomed up through the mist and rain, he leaned forward in his seat. Half to himself, half to his driver, Wilson, he observed, 'I might even have to wear the kilt.'

Wilson's eyes widened. He tightened his grip on the steering wheel and swallowed hard. Christ, the Colonel in a kilt! He stabbed his foot down on the accelerator and the car leaped forward.

Past the Glen Nevis distillery and Inverlochy Castle. On through the wide open country of the great glen to Spean Bridge, where the car turned left and the engine revved to take the hill. Left at the fork at the top and on across the lock gates of the Caledonian Canal at Gairlochy to the Banavie road. Then twisting and turning along the narrow, switchback road to Achnacarry.

Through windows against which the rain was beating heavily, Vaughan gazed at the rocky peaks surrounding them. 'It's an 'elluva country,' he announced in his husky voice. As they reached the top of a hill, he caught a glimpse of the imposing house that was to be his castle. Then his car accelerated downwards, slowing to make the turn through the main gates into the tree-lined driveway. Tyres grated on shingle as the car stopped, churning the gravel in front of the house. On the doorstep, a kilted figure was waiting. Vaughan sprang out of the car. His hand went up in a salute.

''Ow are you, Sir? I'm Charles Vaughan.'

Sir Donald Walter Cameron of Lochiel acknowledged the salute Highland fashion, lifting his stick and raising two fingers.

He was dressed in tweeds and tartan, with scuffed brogues on his feet. It was obvious he was used to being in the open and loved to tramp through his hills. A pair of mild grey eyes considered Vaughan from a deeply tanned, weather-beaten face.

It was a historic moment.

Not since the Duke of Cumberland in 1745 had an English soldier and his troops occupied Achnacarry. On that occasion, they had burned and ravaged the place. Now Vaughan was taking possession. His troops would follow. What would they do to Achnacarry in 1942?

From far and near, in the great cities of the world and in lonely outposts, the Camerons looked to Achnacarry. Lochiel was not only their chief, the head of their clan and family, he was their trustee, to hold, maintain, and keep forever the ties and associations, the ground and policies. And now, all this was to be at the mercy of an English soldier.

True, Lochiel would not be far away. He would be taking up residence at Clunes, some two miles from Achnacarry. From there, he would be able to keep a weather eye on his estate – and Charles Vaughan.

True also, some of the treasures had been safely locked away. Relics of a bygone age of chivalry and romance. Relics like the silver flask presented to a past Lochiel by Bonnie Prince Charlie in Paris, in 1747. It bore the inscription: 'Snuff box or dram cup, while skulking in ye Highlands.'

What kind of skulking had this strange Sassenach Vaughan in mind for ye Highlands?

Safely locked away, too, was the clan banner. This proud flag had had to be saved once already from the English. After Culloden, MacLachlan of Coruanan, hereditary standard bearer to Lochiel, had smuggled it to safety by wrapping it round his body under his clothes.

11

Also in storage was a claymore which had been wielded by a Cameron at the Battle of Harlaw, and an ancient targe bearing the words: 'Fear God, Honour the King.'

Whether or not the Camerons suspected that the Commandos might be short of weapons, I couldn't say. But a famous old flint-lock which had belonged to Sir Ewan of Lochiel had also been carefully put away. With this weapon, Sir Ewan was said to have killed the last wolf in the Highlands.

Was Lieutenant-Colonel Charles Edward Vaughan about to breed some more?

# 3

**V**AUGHAN'S very first move after taking over at Achnacarry was to try to convince not only the general civilian public – but service chiefs who should have known better in the first place – that the Commandos were not a wild, undisciplined mob of cut-throats, thugs, gangsters, ex-gaolbirds, and what have you. The popular impression of a Commando had hitherto been of someone who would just as soon wreck a peaceful British village as an enemy gun battery, someone who was just as liable to stick a knife into a civvie barman as a German sentry, someone from whom pretty wives and daughters should be safely locked away.

To correct this idea was a crusade of which Vaughan never tired. He even went the length of inviting parties of newspapermen to Achnacarry to see for themselves. It often occurred to me that he could have saved himself a lot of trouble merely by sending me out on tour.

At the outbreak of war I was pursuing a career in banking with the Royal Bank of Scotland. It was an old bank which had been forced to support Bonnie Prince Charlie and his rebel troops to the extent of £3076 when they occupied Edinburgh on their way south, in 1745. Was that prudent, I wondered? Ah well! You win some, you lose some.

I always dressed conservatively in a bowler hat and pin-striped suit. Save for an odd Hogmanay spree my personal conduct reached the high standard of respectability expected by the directors of the bank. True, I played rugger for the Craigielie club with chaps like big Dave McGhee who would join the Royal Engineers, Ian Buchanan, the Royal Navy and Archie McKellar would become an ace fighter pilot in the famous No. 602 City of Glasgow Squadron, the Royal Air Force.

Tough and rugged though some of our matches were, the experience was hardly sufficient for me to fit into the picture the public had formed of the Commandos. Indeed, although I bore the wounds of battle, a broken nose and a broken arm, anyone less like a hell raising desperado than myself would have been hard to find.

13

Nor was I an exceptional case by any means. The Commandos were full of men like me. Plain, ordinary chaps. Butchers, bakers, and – though I can't remember offhand ever having come across any – possibly candlestick makers too. Born Commandos, devil-may-care, swashbuckling characters – like Colonel 'Mad Jack' Churchill, who charged the Germans swinging a cutlass – were few and far between, though they added a welcome dash of colour and glamour. The rest, the vast majority – I would go so far as to say about ninety-nine percent – had to be made. Their only qualifications were fitness, enthusiasm, and a reasonable supply of intelligence.

When Vaughan finally convinced everyone that the Commandos were not hooligans, a fresh misconception arose. The Commandos were now Greek gods, supermen. That one was equally unreal. Commandos came in all shapes and sizes – tall ones, short ones, old ones, young ones, muscular ones, scrawny ones, handsome ones, and downright ugly ones. They were not supermen. They were ordinary men who had been super-*trained* – at Achnacarry.

This may sound like an Army joke, but it's true – I went to Achnacarry direct from a Butlin holiday camp. It was the one at Filey. A captain in the 9th Cameronians (Scottish Rifles), I had been posted there to assist in the organisation of the new R.A.F. Regiment. I wasn't too happy about the move. For one thing, it had meant parting company with a lot of my old Territorial Army friends. Fellows like Arnold Cochran, who owned a draper's business in Paisley, and with whom I had often played tennis in pre-war days.

For another, it was now 1942 and, apart from a dog-fight overhead, I had yet to hear a shot fired in anger. I still cherished the naïve notion that I had joined the Army to fight Germans, not to shove bull down the reluctant throats of R.A.F. erks.

I had applied to join, and been accepted, for service in a Punjab Regiment. It was while I was awaiting word from India Office that I picked up a newspaper in the mess one day and read about the Commando raid on the Lofotens.

It was heartening to realise that I had not been entirely misled by Messrs Samuel Goldwyn, Errol Flynn, and John Wayne after all. Some soldiers actually did fire guns and attack the enemy. My dreams of India faded. I volunteered for the Commandos.

In due course, I made my appearance before a selection board at

Special Brigade Headquarters, which was in a mansion in Ayrshire. My tartan trews had creases like the edge of a razor, my service dress tunic was carefully pressed, my Sam Browne belt shone like patent leather. Glengarry ribbons flying, I marched smartly into a large room with huge bay windows, came to attention as if my life depended on it, and threw a salute that a Sergeant-Major in the Guards would have acclaimed with an admiring oath.

Four officers in battledress lolled languidly in their chairs behind a long table near the window. Like the members of every kind of selection board under the sun, they looked bored and thoroughly uninterested. I thought I saw one of them wince as my heels banged to attention.

Like all selection boards they had a knack of making a man feel that he was something that had just crawled out from under a stone. Despite my bandbox appearance, I squirmed inwardly under their scrutiny.

'Gilchrist?' asked one of them in a lazy Oxford drawl, almost as if he hoped I wasn't – thus ending the whole tedious business.

Then came the questions:

'What sports do you play?'

'Do you drink beer?'

'Can you swim?'

'Do you play any musical instruments?'

'Have you a sex life?'

'Were you a boy scout?'

These and many others I answered as truthfully and clearly as I could, although the purpose of some of the questions was quite beyond me.

At last, I was told that that would be all and that I could go. I left the room in what seemed to me an atmosphere of mutual relief that it was all over.

I hadn't the slightest inkling as to whether I'd made a favourable impression or otherwise. Indeed, I doubted if I'd made any impression on the selection board at all. And I feared the worst.

Nevertheless, I was accepted. Within a fortnight, I was on my way home for seven days' leave. When it ended, I was to report to a place called Achnacarry.

For the first time since I'd joined up, a week's leave actually seemed to drag. I was secretly rather glad when I discovered I'd have to leave home a day early. The only suitable train to Spean Bridge left Queen Street Station, Glasgow, at the deserted hour of 5.45 a.m. I would have to spend the previous night at a hotel in Glasgow to be sure of catching it. Even at that, I had a shrewd suspicion that the night porter would have to work overtime – and would certainly earn his tip – getting me up in time.

I said my good-byes on the doorstep of our home in Kingsburgh Drive; to my father, mother, and sister. My older brother was in the Royal Engineers.

In cold print, my mother's send-off may seem extremely commonplace. 'Donald,' she said hesitantly, 'don't be angry with me for saying this. But look after yourself – and don't get your feet wet.'

Her words came back to me many a time at Achnacarry, mostly when I was splashing and staggering through waist-deep water. But I recalled them with no great sense of irony. It was a comfort to know that at least one person in the world cared whether I got my feet wet or not. The Commandos certainly didn't!

I spent the night in the Ivanhoe Hotel in Buchanan Street, a stone's throw from Queen Street Station. The night porter proved a master in the art of banging on bedroom doors. I had time to wash, shave, and breakfast on tea and toast before setting out for the station. *En route*, I found myself squinting self-consciously and somewhat sadly at my shoulders. Until recently, three pips had stood there proudly, side by side. Now there were only two.

It was a condition of acceptance that all ranks volunteering for Special Service had to revert to their war substantive rank. I was now a lieutenant. Such was the cost of becoming a Commando. I felt naked without that third pip. Even at that, my sacrifice was a relatively small one. Sergeant-Majors voluntarily became privates, just to get into the Commandos, a truth which even Ripley might find too much to believe or not.

My train was standing at platform 9, with the engine having a quiet smoke to fortify itself for the efforts that lay ahead. I strolled up the platform in search of the first-class accommodation – nonchalantly used by all Army officers with free warrants. In passing, I glanced through the windows of some of the third-class compartments. A wild confusion of Army boots, stockinged feet, bodies, braces, bayonets, unbuttoned khaki tunics, packs, pouches, and rifles filled every available cubic inch of space. Clearly, the Commando clan was gathering.

By comparison, the first-class compartments seemed almost deserted. I had no difficulty in finding a window seat.

There were only two other occupants. A naval officer was sprawled out in one corner, snoring. A Wren officer sat, eyes closed, in another. As I entered, she peeked through her eyelashes at me. But having observed that I was not an admiral, she closed her eyes again. Shortly after the train had jolted its way out of the station, I fell asleep myself.

I was awakened by a porter yelling 'Crianlarich! Crianlarich!'

The naval officer seemed to be a submariner. He had not yet surfaced. The trim little craft in the other corner was having a refit with lipstick and mirror. I lowered a window and looked out. A terrific scrum had formed round a door marked 'Refreshments.' Tea!

I managed to collect three cups and careful threaded my way back to the compartment with them. The Wren signalled her thanks with her eyelashes. The submariner came up to recharge his batteries.

From Crianlarich the train climbed steadily northwards, through scenery that became increasingly wilder and more forbidding. By Tyndrum and Bridge of Orchy, over bleak Rannoch Moor, and on past Loch Treig. A pitiless drizzle was falling as the train finally rumbled down a slight gradient and clanged and clattered to a halt at a picturesque little station.

Above the hiss of steam, I could hear the sound of the pipes and – like a ghostly echo of the '45 – a porter shouting in a high-pitched, Highland voice: 'Spee…ann Prri…dge!' The station became a hive of activity as the train disgorged its khaki cargo, through which a kilted Pipe Major went swinging up and down playing a quickstep.

It was easy to pick out the instructors from Achnacarry. They wore camouflaged rainproof jackets. Their boots and faces shone. Their brasses were beaten flat and burnished. And they were giving orders.

I reported to an officer, as did three other fellow trainee officers from various parts of the train. We exchanged the customary stiff glances and casual nods. As the engine gave a farewell blast and began to pull away, officers and other ranks were herded over the bridge through the rain. I heard a sigh or two of relief as some of the troops spotted some lorries. Relief changed to vague suspicion as it was seen that kit bags only were being loaded aboard them.

Some one summoned up enough courage to ask an N.C.O.: 'Is it far? Do we get transport?'

His reply rattled out like a Bren gun burst. 'Not far. Seven miles. No transport.'

17

Seven miles – in this rain! There was a lot of moaning and groaning as we formed up. Then, headed and flanked by instructors, off we went. The piper was playing a tune that would have made the dead get up and march – which, in our case, was almost essential. The instructors looked as if they were out to enjoy a short stroll. We – as someone muttered at the time – looked as if we were about to march seven bloody miles through the bloody rain.

Past Spean Bridge Hotel, through the village to the bridge, and over the river. On and on we marched until our boots drummed on the bridge over the Caledonian Canal. Then up a back-bending, stamina-sapping incline. We climbed so much, I began to wonder if the hills in this part of the country went up on both sides.

Civilisation was fast becoming just a memory. There were no houses to be seen now. No sign of cultivation. Just hills, bracken, trees, and the rain – the ceaseless, soaking rain.

My trousers were sodden and stuck to my legs. The water ran off my gas cape in torrents. I looked at the faces of those marching beside me. They were washed clean of everything but expressions of misery, and red with the exertion of the march. Cap badges of many different regiments sparkled with beads of rain.

But the men had one great consolation. 'At least the bloody officers have got to walk as well!'

Although I've no doubt that it tried its best, the march couldn't last forever. At last, Achnacarry House loomed into view. A magnificent building – four good walls and a roof. It would, without question, be dry inside.

We were halted just inside the main gate. Somehow or other, I summoned up the strength to raise my head and look around me. Everywhere I looked, soldiers were on the move. Some were doubling here and there in squads, N.C.O.s barking at them like collies chasing on sheep. Others were drilling under Guards sergeants – easily recognised by their pace sticks, and their voices. Outside the camp, more men were crawling up an almost perpendicular rock face like khaki flies.

Then I saw the graves. There was a long row of them alongside the trees that lined the driveway. They were marked by white crosses. Nailed to each cross was a small board bearing a number, rank, and name, under which was given the cause of death. I could read the two nearest me.

'He showed himself on the skyline.'

'He failed to take cover in an assault landing.'

I felt like chuckling, but somehow I couldn't quite make it. The graves were phoney, of course... Or, were they?

Evidently the others had noticed the graves to. And at least one man shared my misgivings. He gestured at the row of crosses and said to an instructor: 'Come off it. Who do you think you're kidding?'

The instructor did not reply. Instead, he gave the trainee a look that seemed to say, 'What kind of a remark is that to make in the presence of the dead?'

We all fell into a strange, nervous silence. If someone was trying to put the fear of death into us, he had undeniably succeeded. Exactly what kind of a place was this? What had we let ourselves in for?

I, for one, was not long in finding out. That night, for the first time in my life, I slept in a castle. It was not quite so luxurious as it may sound. The room was cold, cheerless, and sparsely furnished. I shared it with three other officers.

Castle or no castle, reveille next morning was at 06.30 hours. No batman with my morning cup of tea. Life at Achnacarry ran on simple lines. So simple, indeed, that one did not even have to ponder on which tap to turn in the bathroom. Both gave forth cold water.

Over a breakfast of porridge and milk, followed by fried bread and bacon, I became better acquainted with some of my fellow trainee officers. There was a magnificently built fellow called Whitfield who had been in the Life Guards. An Irishman called Sullivan. Jimmy James from Wales. And to add a final international touch, two Englishmen, Hobson and Ruxton.

The Adjutant, a sharp-featured captain whose name, inappropriately enough, was Joy, came in and told us to report to the Orderly Room at 09.00 hours. We did so, and were marched in for an audience with the new Laird of Achnacarry, Lieutenant-Colonel Charles Edward Vaughan.

He sat there inspecting us closely as we surveyed him – and certainly a lot more openly. The chair was entirely filled by his bulk. His face was florid, but fit-looking. His chin was square. His eyes were pale blue. His hair was greying, and there wasn't much of it. With what there was he had done his best, and you would not have called him bald. His voice was throaty. His manner was fatherly.

'I'm very sorry about this,' he began, 'but we haven't enough officers here to run a proper course this time. What we are going to do is to give you some special training for a week, then you will officer the men going through their course.'

He blew his nose with a huge coloured handkerchief and continued: 'We work hard here at Achnacarry.' He paused, but nobody tried to argue that point. 'We expect you to set an example and to lead the men as you will have to do when you go to a Command.' His massive head went back, and he raised his eyebrows. 'We have no batmen for trainee officers. You have to clean your own equipment.'

He leaned forward and inquired in confidential tones: 'How can you tell if a man has had time to clean his belt and gaiters if you haven't done it yourself?' He cleared his throat. 'Now then,' he went on briskly, 'I've laid on a very nice day to break you in to Achnacarry. The Mess Sergeant has made up some haversack rations. You will take the ration truck to Fort William.'

Pressing his palms against the table, he pushed himself back against his chair. 'You will then climb Ben Nevis,' he rapped out. 'Any questions?'

We were stunned. No hot water. No batmen. And now – Ben Nevis!

Sullivan recovered first. 'Sir, and when will we be catching the truck *back* from Fort William?' A wonderful question. Thank God for an Irishman.

The Colonel's fatherly look vanished abruptly. An expression of outraged amazement took its place. He seemed unable to believe his own ears.

'Transport? Transport?' he gasped weakly. 'Good God!'

He glared at the unfortunate Sullivan. 'Look 'ere,' he said, 'what you want is your ears pinned back.' Then he inspected us all carefully, one by one. 'Here I am,' he continued plaintively. 'I've done my best to help you. I lay on a very pleasant day on Ben Nevis. You'll like that hill. It belongs to Lockiel and he's very proud of it. But all you can think of is transport.'

Dismissing us with an impatient gesture, he added: 'Never heard anything like it. Only eighteen miles, and you 'owl for transport...'

# 4

WHATEVER else it lacked, my first week as a Commando didn't lack variety. We climbed Ben Nevis, and – despite our 'howl for transport' – walked the eighteen miles back to Achnacarry. My feet were still aching at breakfast the next morning when Ben Hoare, one of the officer instructors, informed us with a rather sadistic smile: 'You're on the assault course this morning.'

But first we were handed over to C.S.M. Robertson for a period of instruction on how to fire foreign weapons. The guns had been captured on previous Commando raids. Like all Vaughan's instructors, Robertson knew his stuff. We could hardly tear ourselves away from him. We liked him. We liked his foreign weapons.

And we had a vague but horrible suspicion of what was to follow…

We reported to Hoare at the appointed hour. He was waiting for us. That was another characteristic of Vaughan's instructors – they had an irritating habit of showing up. The assault course, too, was waiting. And it was raining. As I later learned, a popular saying amongst Commandos was: 'It always rains at Achnacarry.'

Hoare took us for a leisurely stroll round the course to begin with. Doubtless he meant well. But it struck me as being rather like taking the condemned man on a tour of inspection of the gallows.

Quite apart from the various obstacles, the very ground itself looked treacherous and formidable enough. It was sodden with rain and slippery. The water ran in a network of tiny rivulets. Between bracken and heather was a morass of a peat bog. Here and there, bare rocks showed greasily through.

The preview was soon over. Stop watch in hand, Hoare sent us off one at a time. I stood there, torn between my reluctance to tackle it at all, and desire to get it over with as soon as possible.

My turn came. Hoare gave me a nod. 'Go!'

I went. Down a slope I hared, my boots churning up mud and water. I made a slithering dive under the first obstacle – a barbed wire fence laid flat. Crawling like a snake, I reached the other side, my denims soaking and my face covered in slimy peat.

Ahead lay a long tree trunk, stripped of its branches, sloping up to a rock outcrop on a hill. You paid your money and you took your choice. Either you dashed recklessly up it, throwing all caution aside and risking a nasty fall. Or you crawled up it, thus losing valuable time.

Remembering the stop watch, I had a go – successfully. As a reward, I had to climb the rest of the rock face. Sweating and panting, I reached the top and pelted on to the gully.

This was a little gorge where, by catching the end of a rope tied to a tree, you could slide down another rock face and over to the other side in one movement. I made it, but had neither the breath nor the inclination to yell like Tarzan.

A tough scramble up to a marked tree, then I turned and went tearing down a steep slope, leaping over rocks, fallen trees, and little streams. This wasn't an assault course – it was the Grand National! The impetus of my run carried me with ten-league strides and rattling equipment to a wooden bridge over a burn. On the other side a small mound reared up in front of me.

This was the home stretch. I made my dying effort. Chest heaving, eyes popping, I staggered and stumbled to the top. A line of dummies stood there as if mocking me.

I hated the sight of them. My blood was up. I lunged at a dummy with fixed bayonet. My mouth opened as my lungs wheezed to give air to a terrifying battle cry. It turned out to be a feeble whisper. Gritting my teeth, I thrust forward the bayonet viciously determined to stick it right through that damned dummy. I didn't even dent the canvas.

Disappointed as I was, I consoled myself with the thought that, at least, the whole business was over and done with.

The figure of Hoare appeared. 'Oh, but you'll have to do better than that,' he said. 'Take a breather and you can try again in a minute.'

I tried again. So did the others. Then we tried it again. We did it until I felt I could have gone over that assault course blindfold.

But, of course, I didn't say so. I had a nasty suspicion that anyone who said a thing like that at Achnacarry was simply asking to have a handkerchief tied round his eyes!

The following day we met the Moon. It was a memorable occasion.

Think of Jeeves in uniform and you will have some idea of Company

Sergeant-Major Moon, the head cook at Achnacarry. Moon had the same air of omniscience, the same precise, rather patronising mode of address, the same dry humour.

In addition to cooking for the staff and trainees at Achnacarry, Moon had been pressed into service as an instructor by Vaughan. He gave lessons on survival – how to live off the land, and cook your food with only the most primitive of equipment.

Moon revelled in this extra duty. He was a born lecturer.

The great man held court in a clearing surrounded by tall beech trees near the castle. When we arrived for his demonstration, a large number of instructors were already waiting. They stood there like spectators at a football match, easily outnumbering our small class. I couldn't quite understand it. Surely they had better things to do in their spare time? Moon certainly must be worth watching to have so many faithful fans.

A swarthy, dark-eyed man, the Moon stood in the centre of the arena. He was surrounded by a Heath Robinson assortment of cookers, cunningly built from heaps of stones, biscuit tins, and various types of tin cans. The scent of burning pine filled the clearing. Smoke and flame spluttered from a small open fire beside him.

With the poised, graceful movements of a sculptor, Moon was kneading clay round a small animal. The animal was already half-covered by the time we arrived. He addressed us in the manner of a head waiter – in tones that were deferential, yet managed to convey the impression that we should be proud to have the honour of his personal attention.

'You take the animal, gentlemen, and press the clay firmly round it as I am doing now. In your wisdom, you will doubtless note that it is a simple task. A child could do it. With diligence, you should manage all right.'

All the time he was talking, he was moulding the clay effortlessly around it. We watched fascinated as he moved to the fire and knelt beside it, like a wizard about to work a spell.

'When you have completed the kneading, so that the entire animal is totally and amply covered, you then rake the open fire and deposit your handiwork reverently in the centre. You will, I trust, be careful to arrange the sticks so as to maintain a constant heat.'

Having placed the mass of clay on the fire, he rose and, with another of his head-waiter gestures, conducted us to further sights.

After initiating us into the art of prehistoric cooking for about half-an-hour, he took us back to the fire. He affected to remember the animal in the clay suddenly, with a surprised raise of his eyebrows.

'Ah,' said the Moon, 'it should be nicely done now.'

Scooping away the embers with a flourish, he extracted the lump of clay – now baked hard – and cracked it open. The two halves he laid flat for our inspection.

We crowded around. It was a masterly job. The fur and skin had remained attached to the clay. The isolated flesh was nicely browned in places. It smelled good, and it looked good.

Like a chef, Moon cut the flesh into succulent morsels which he arranged attractively on a plate. Like a butler, he offered the plate to each of us in turn. We each took a piece and ate it with much enjoyment. It had a pleasant, if rather strong taste.

'Now then, gentlemen, I should like, if I may, to ask you a question,' said Sergeant Moon. 'What flesh was that?'

'Rabbit, sergeant?' ventured someone.

'Hare, sergeant?' queried someone else.

The moon smiled indulgently. 'Oh, come now, gentlemen, think again.'

'Squirrel?' I suggested, without much confidence.

Moon shook his head, rather sadly. 'I'm afraid I shall have to contradict you.'

He paused significantly at this point, and all the spectating instructors closed in – as if something special was about to happen.

It did. A faintly superior smile on his face, the Moon announced in soft, silky tones: 'That, gentlemen, was Achnacarry Rat!'

In the race to be sick into the river, I came in a close second.

Nevertheless, the Moon was a handy man to have around. We were given ample proof of this on the very last day of our course.

With Whitfield in charge, we were sent on a speed march, with rifles and equipment, to a point in Glen Mallie and back – a total distance of eight miles.

A speed march is similar to the Boy Scouts' run-and-walk, only tuned up to Silverstone standards. Even if nothing else had happened, I would have remembered the march merely for the fact that it was not raining. But something else did happen.

It was almost bound to happen. Before setting out, we held a private conference. The countryside around the castle abounded in game. Why not have a crack at some of it?

When we trotted out of the camp gates with Whitfield in the lead, each of us had five rounds of .303 ammunition tucked away in a pocket of his denims. I had visions of a magnificent stag's head adorning the hall of my household. I could see myself coming home at night and nonchalantly tossing my hat on to one of the antlers.

Whitfield was fit, and bursting with energy and enthusiasm – which was probably why he'd been put in charge of us. He set a cracking pace. We marched up hills, ran down them, and divided the level ground to suit our wind. By the time we reached Inver Mallie, just over two miles away, my dreams of a stag and antlers had dissolved in the sweat of exertion.

We crossed the bridge over the River Mallie and turned into the track through the glen. It was a long, deeply-cut, lonely valley, with hills sweeping up on either side of the river. After we'd been following the truck for about ten minutes, Whitfield stopped so suddenly that the rest of us crowded up on to him.

'Christ!' someone whispered hoarsely.

A herd of deer was grazing, no more than two hundred yards away.

The others threw themselves to the ground, rammed home their five rounds of .303, and began firing indiscriminately and inaccurately. The deer kicked up their hoofs and fled in panic.

'Cease firing,' said an authoritative voice. I recognised it, with some surprise, as my own. As the others looked at me expectantly, I went on: 'Sights up, 250, single stag on small mound.'

It is a curious feature of deer that, after their initial panic, they will stop and not move again until certain of the exact point from which they are being attacked. The herd had halted, poised for their final flight.

The stag was standing apart from the rest on a slight rise in the ground. It stood there with its head up, staring at us as if trying to anticipate our next move. There was a proud defiance in its attitude. It was the leader of the herd. To show fear would be beneath its dignity.

Five rifles were carefully aimed. I gave my final order: 'Fire!'

Five shots sounded almost as one. The herd vanished in a flurry of hoofs and flying turf. But the hero who had drawn our fire lay dead. Racing over, we looked down at our prize – first with pride at our own prowess, then with remorse at having killed so magnificent a beast.

Our excitement evaporated at an astonishing rate. We stopped looking at the stag and started looking at each other – and around about us – uneasily. The thrill of the hunter had been replaced by – the stigma of the poacher!

This was Lochaber. Cameron country. Everything belonged to the Camerons, whether it grew out of the ground, ran about on top of it, or flew in the air above it. Lochiel and his ghillies might have something to say about a deer being murdered by a bunch of trigger-happy trainee Commando officers. And there was that other fine Highland gentleman to worry about – Colonel Charles MacVaughan!

Whitfield finally spoke up.

'I'd better run back for a truck.'

We looked at him dumbly.

'Well, what are you waiting for?' asked Jimmy James.

'Christ,' commented Whitfield, 'there's not much competition for the job with you fellows!'

But off he went, back in the direction of the Castle, at the double. I found myself in charge of the situation. As Whitfield had said, there wasn't a great deal of competition. I was now stuck with one dead deer and four other rather jittery apprentice poachers.

'We'll have to camouflage the body, and we'd better post a couple of scouts,' I said. As two of them left to take up positions on the track on either side of the fateful scene, I added: 'Pretend you're map reading.'

The rest of us began cutting bracken as if our lives depended on it. In no time at all, we had the stag covered. We had it covered so thoroughly that a passer-by would almost certainly have been attracted to the spot just to find out what was underneath the heap of bracken.

'How are we going to carry it?' someone asked. There seemed to be no end to the problems of amateur deer poachers.

We held a long consultation. Eventually it was decided to adopt the method used by native tribes to carry their kills back to the village. We would cut a strong sapling, thread a couple of pull-throughs through the tendons behind the hoofs of the deer, tie the pull-throughs to the sapling, and carry the sapling on our shoulders.

Hobson suggested bleeding the stag to reduce the weight. Again there was no competition for the job. Much to everyone's relief, I pointed out that the blood would leave a mess in the truck. That settled the matter. No bleeding.

Jimmy James cut a sapling, and stripped off all the small branches. I asked 'Hobbie' if he had his pull-through. He looked in the butt of his rifle. His expression showed surprise. He had it.

We cut the tendons with our bayonets, threaded the pull-throughs into place, looped the ends over the sapling, and tied them securely. Everything was ready. All we had to do was wait for Whitfield.

Our two scouts were still at their posts – map-reading assiduously. Suddenly one of them began to signal frantically, and we heard the sound of a motor engine. It was Whitfield, with a truck.

Before I could ask him by what Commando tactics he had acquired it, he started giving orders. I relinquished my command gladly.

'Right now,' said Whitfield briskly. 'Everybody lend a hand and we'll have it on the truck in a jiffy.'

Everybody did lend a hand, but the affair was not over in a jiffy. The sapling idea was all right in theory. But we had underestimated the weight of the deer. When we tried to get it on to our shoulders, the sapling bent like a bow.

The erstwhile 'noble animal' became a 'bloody thing!' We pulled, shoved, heaved, and lifted it over the 300-odd yards from where it had been shot to where the lorry was parked at the side of the track. Over bracken and bog the strange scene was enacted. We staggered, stumbled, cursed, and sweated.

But, at last, we made it. The still warm body was hoisted up and tucked into the back of the truck. Then we all clambered aboard and drove off.

As we went bowling along the road back towards the Castle, Jimmy James asked what he must have felt was a not unreasonable question: 'Look here – what the hell are we going to do with it now?'

All of a sudden, the cigarettes we had been enjoying after our exertions did not taste so sweet. There was a long silence, broken only by occasional outbursts of strained, idiotic laughter.

Then, Sullivan had a brainwave. 'Lochiel has a deer pit this side of the Castle. I've seen it. Why not put it in there? After all, it's *his* deer.' The Irishman would think of it that way!

It would be like hiding a body in the grounds of Scotland Yard. The operation would have to be carried out right under Vaughan's nose – a nose that could smell out a scrap of paper in the remotest corner of the camp during inspections. The whole idea was completely crazy. Yet, we adopted it. Nobody could think of a better one.

When the moment came, the deer was hauled out of the truck a lot more quickly than it had been loaded aboard. The incident must have been reminiscent of a scene from a Keystone Cops comedy. No sooner had the wheels of the truck scrunched to a stop on the gravel than we all piled out and went frantically to work. Down came the back of the truck. Out came the deer. Into the pit it was bundled. And off went Whitfield to return the truck.

He rejoined us in a minute or two at a prearranged rendezvous, and we held another conference. How were we going to make our official entry into the camp?

'Sure, a speed march we started, and a speed march we'll finish. And if we look tired enough, no one will be asking what we did in between.'

It was Sullivan again. I looked at him in open admiration. The man was a genius. He would do well in the Army.

We sneaked back through the woods to the bridge at Arkaig, then about turned and went back towards the camp at the double. We were puffing and blowing when we reached the main gate. Anyone could see that we'd been on a tough march. The highlight of our performance came outside the Adjutant's office, where we swayed slightly as we stood to attention waiting for Whitfield to dismiss us.

Upstairs in the Castle, we plunged into cold baths with subdued glee. We'd got away with it – up to a point. But we still had to dispose of the body. Neither Lochiel nor Vaughan was likely to assume that the deer in question had crawled into the pit and died.

As Bertie Wooster turns to Jeeves in times of stress, we turned to the Moon...

The sequel came at dinner in the Officers' Mess the following evening. Vaughan was in good humour, and had insisted that the trainee officers should sit near him.

'Well, how are you liking it up here at Acknacarry, eh?' he demanded genially. 'Enjoy your speed march yesterday?'

The arrival of the meat course absolved us from making any immediate reply. As we ate the roast beef, peas and potatoes, we did our best to change the subject and get him on to his stories – of which he had an inexhaustible supply.

He was entertaining with a highly amusing anecdote of his early Army days, when the waiter approached with a large serving plate on which there was a liberal amount of meat. This struck me as rather unusual. Second helpings of meat were rare at Achnacarry.

'A little more meat, sir?' said the waiter. Without waiting for a reply, he quickly dealt a portion on to the Colonel's plate and passed on to us.

I looked at what was on the Colonel's plate. I studied what was later deposited on my own. It wasn't roast beef...

No, it couldn't be. Not even Sergeant Moon would have the nerve.

Then I noticed my companions exchanging furtive, frightened glances. It *was*!

Colonel Vaughan cut a piece, raised it to his mouth and sampled it. Abruptly, he stopped chewing. A thoughtful expression came over his face.

It was a tense moment. Had he recognised the taste of venison? He had been an R.S.M. in the Guards, therefore he knew everything about everything. Was he at this very moment working out every conceivable route by which venison could have arrived on his plate? Venison came from deer. Who had had the freedom of movement, the opportunity – who would be misguided enough, stupid enough – to kill a deer? Was my instinct away off the beam, or had he, in those few split seconds, reconstructed all that had happened during and after our historic speed march? Was it possible, on the other hand, that he suspected nothing? We waited anxiously, breathlessly.

Suddenly, the Colonel's jaws started to move again. He chewed. He swallowed. He took another piece.

We exchanged smiles of relief. That master cook and master-mind, the Moon, had done it. We were in the clear.

Lieutenant-Colonel Charles Edward Vaughan was an accessory after the fact!

# 5

OUR short but concentrated officers' course was over. As Vaughan had told us on arrival, we would now have to act as instructors to the men for a time. The Colonel reminded us of this with the words: 'It'll do you good. You don't want to hang about camp lying on your bed and drinking beer. What you want to do is get out into the hills and get yourselves fit.'

From which we gathered that Colonel Vaughan was of the opinion that our week of training had been in the nature of a rest cure. I could have indignantly told him otherwise – if I'd had the guts. I hadn't. Neither had any of the rest of us. So we said nothing.

Every aspect of the training at Achnacarry was tough. The course varied only inasmuch as some types of training were even tougher than others. For the latter, Vaughan shrewdly paired off his new boys with more experienced instructors. I was taken under the somewhat unconventional wing of an officer called Alick Cowieson who was, as our American friends colourfully put it: 'A wild man from 'way back.'

He was a tall, broad-shouldered Highlander who wore the tartan of the Cameron Highlanders. His dark hair was thinning. The skin of his face, drawn tight over the bones, shone as though polished. His eyes were dark and had the very devil in them. When he smiled, you could see that many of his teeth were missing. I never had the nerve to ask him how he lost his teeth. I had a suspicion that the explanation would be one that would keep me awake at nights.

Alick was the chief Macchiavelli of Achnacarry. As well as being an instructor, that wild brain of his was always dreaming up fresh terrors for the unfortunate trainees. I was actually with him on the day he gave birth to his most famous – or infamous – brainwave. The 'Death Ride'.

With excitement he could barely suppress, Alick – I had secretly christened him 'Alick Mor' meaning in Gaelic 'Alick the Mighty' – conducted Company Quartermaster Sergeant Frickleton and myself down to the River Arkaig. Frickleton was the chief P.T. instructor. He was a small compact bundle of muscles with a head of closely cropped curls and a well-developed sense of humour.

Alick Mor was equipped with a long climbing rope and a short toggle rope.

The toggle rope was a curious but useful item of Commando equipment. About four feet in length, it had a piece of wood at one end and a loop at the other. It was a simple matter to thread the wood through the loop. The toggle rope could then be used in a variety of ways.

Several could be joined together to make a chain. It could be used individually as an aid in scaling walls. Or many of them could be interlaced to form a toggle bridge strong enough to support half-a-dozen or more fully-equipped men at a time.

In this latter role, the toggle rope had already become a familiar Achnacarry landmark. A toggle bridge, strung high between tall beech trees on either bank, crossed the River Arkaig – ironically enough only a matter of yards upriver from an iron footbridge.

Crossing the toggle bridge was by no means easy. It was a common – and much appreciated – sight to see trainees performing all sorts of unintentional acrobatics on it. One slip and anyone crossing found himself entangled upside-down in a mesh of rope. The more he struggled and writhed, the worse his predicament became – until, finally, a yell and a mighty splash signalled the inevitable outcome. The waters of the Arkaig were icy cold, so that the unfortunate ones received a most unpleasant ducking. Normally such incidents provided an amusing interlude in the training. But two lives had been lost on the toggle bridge.

The Arkaig was in spate at the time, but no one thought of the river as being treacherous. One moment five men were carefully picking their way over the bridge – the next, all five were in the river. In the general confusion, two of the men were swept away by the current unnoticed. They may have been stunned. They may have been poor swimmers. Whatever the reason, their bodies were later recovered almost at Loch Lochy. From that day on, a grapple net was suspended from the footbridge as a safety measure.

The toggle bridge, however, wasn't nearly dangerous enough for Alick Mor. He had evolved a hair-raising variation of the theme. As we walked down to the river, he gave us the broad outlines of his scheme.

31

One end of his climbing rope he proposed to tie to the top of a tree on one bank of the Arkaig. The other end would be attached to the base of a tree on the opposite bank of the river. The rope was then pulled taut. Alick – and future generations of luckless trainees – would then loop a trusty toggle rope over the climbing rope and zoom down from the top of the tree on one bank to the base of the tree on the other. A distance of fifty feet from tree to tree as the crow flies, and a height of between thirty and forty feet above the River Arkaig – as the Commando falls.

After a careful inspection of all convenient timber, Alick selected an ancient pylon of a tree. Tying one end of the climbing rope to his belt, Alick hauled himself laboriously up into the topmost branches, while Frickleton and I waited expectantly below.

Up in the forest something stirred. 'All right, take the other end of the rope across the river and tie it to the foot of a tree,' Alick bellowed. 'Stretch it as tight as you can.'

Frickleton and I saved ourselves from wet feet by borrowing an idea from the Clyde steamers. We tied a long piece of string to the end of the rope, and crossed the footbridge with the rope in tow. On the other side, we yanked on the rope until it was as taut as we could make it, then tied it to the base of a tree – directly opposite to the one in which Alick was perched. It looked perfect. There was a small landing platform on our side for those who came slithering down.

Over on the other side, Alick was busy with his toggle rope. He threaded the wooden peg through the loop, thus making a complete circle of rope. This he placed across the rope stretching over the river so that two loops dropped on either side of it. He then put his wrists through the loops, twisted them securely, and held on to the toggle rope above them. A kick with his feet against the trunk of the tree – and he was off on his Achnacarry-made breeches buoy.

Frickleton and I held our breaths as he sailed down the rope. Such a thing had never been seen before. Everything depended on the ropes. For the first second or so, all went well. Alick came soaring down merrily. But we hadn't managed to pull the rope taut enough. It sagged in the middle, bringing Alick's progress to a halt and leaving him suspended over the middle of the river by his wrists.

It was a sticky situation. I couldn't see what he was going to do about it. His weight had fastened the twisted toggle rope into handcuffs around his wrists. Even if he did manage to release them, the best he could hope for was a drop into the river.

But Alick Mor, the man of many ideas, wasn't beaten. He began to swing himself back and forth with the motion of a pendulum. Every time his knees came up, he kicked out vigorously with his legs. The toggle rope was thus jerked along the line inch by inch. The process required an almost superhuman effort. Alick's eyes were bulging, his mouth was working, his breathing was noisy, and occasionally his tongue popped out of the corner of his mouth. I found myself thinking that it was a good thing he hadn't many teeth. I couldn't take my eyes off his face. Determination, the will to win was written all over his contorted features. Bit by bit he closed the gap. It seemed as though he'd make it to the bank without getting his feet wet.

I looked at Frickleton. Frickleton looked at me. We were thinking the same thing. We'd never have such an opportunity again.

'Hold on, sir!' yelled Frickleton. 'We'll let you down!'

'Stick it, Alick!' I shouted. 'We'll help you!'

And we both began to loosen the rope at the base of the tree.

A string of oaths came across the river. Our parentage was discussed right back to Adam. But Frickleton and I pretended not to hear and went on with our 'rescue' work, yelling reassuringly when he yelled, to drown him out. Despairingly, he increased his swing. He had nearly made it when – splash! There was a spout of water in the Arkaig. Then a red, irate face appeared above the surface, hair straggling over it, dripping wet, spitting water, and mouthing revenge. It was an awesome sight.

Frickleton and I had seen enough. We were off. Over the bridge, through the trees, up the avenue, and over the assault course we raced – taking the obstacles in our stride – with Alick in hot pursuit. At last we reached the Castle, spent with exhaustion and laughter.

It cost us half-a-dozen whiskies to dry him out and dampen his wrath. But the 'Death Ride' was there to stay. The rope, when drawn taut, made an excellent pulley down which literally thousands of trainees travelled at top speed. And not only at Achnacarry. The Yanks came, saw, and copied it for training courses back in the United States.

The aforementioned C.Q.M.S. Frickleton had a streak of inventive genius in him too. He had designed a test that made even the stoutest trainee's heart quail – the 'Tarzan Course'.

Not far from Alick's 'Death Ride' there stood a long line of tall majestic beech trees. The trees had been planted by the 'Gentle Lochiel' in 1745. Indeed, legend has it that he was in the midst of planting them when the news was brought to him that Bonnie Prince Charlie had raised his standard. A gentle man by nature, as his title implies, Lochiel had hurriedly finished his planting and hastened off to warn the Prince against what seemed to him a reckless, ill-timed enterprise.

He would probably have shuddered with horror at the use to which Frickleton had put his trees. For a stretch of about fifty yards, the uppermost branches were festooned with ropes, as if some gigantic spider had woven a web. At heights of between thirty to forty feet, these ropes led from tree to tree, spanning gaps of from fifteen to twenty feet. They were used for training the men in cat-crawling – that is to say crawling along with the torso flat on a single strand of rope. One leg was extended backwards and the top of the foot curled over the rope, the other leg dangling down to maintain balance. The cat-crawler pulled himself along the line, his leg going like a piston behind him.

At intervals there were wooden platforms – but not for resting. The loose end of a rope was conveniently placed near each platform, the other end being tied to a branch at a greater height. Across a space a grappling net was strung out. The idea was to swing out from the platform, let go, and grab the grappling net. What with climbing, cat-crawling, and swinging, the trainee Commando had to give a pretty fair imitation of a monkey on the 'Tarzan Course'.

Even Frickleton had never been able to cover the whole course in one effort – and he was a superb physical specimen. As can be readily understood, though doled out in small doses, the course was pretty strong medicine for the average trainee. A trainee like Jimmy, for example.

That may not have been his name. His name isn't all that important, anyway. In the history of the Achnacarry 'Tarzan Course' there were quite a few trainees like Jimmy. He was a member of a troop I saw going through part of the course during my first week as an instructor. A giant was in charge of the troop. A six-foot six-inch giant naked to the waist, rippling with muscles and deeply tanned, wearing the black training trousers used by the P.T. staff. A pair of boxing boots on his feet, he moved with the silence and grace of a panther. He was Sergeant Bissell, an ex-policeman.

Every member of the troop had completed the test except Jimmy. His head hanging, his face pale, he had refused to do it. Bissell wasn't raving. He was speaking to him quietly, giving him one last chance. 'All you have to do is climb up there, do that cat-crawl, and come down. I'll be up with you to help you.'

Jimmy mumbled an inaudible reply. The rest of the troop were silent. Bissell kept on talking. 'Your troop will lose marks in the inter-troop competition.' He paused. 'This will count against you. You might be R.T.U.d' Another pause. 'You know what that means? Returned to your unit.' He paused even longer, watching the lad wrestling with his fear, then added, 'They've all done it but you.'

Jimmy's features were twisted. He shifted from one foot to the other. Suddenly he swallowed hard, nodded his head, and made for the rope. Bissell was right behind him. Up and up they climbed, with Jimmy glancing down nervously from time to time. When they reached the branch where the line began, Bissell had to encourage him before he would tackle the cat-crawl. I could hear him giving his instructions calmly and tonelessly.

After a couple of false starts, Jimmy was out on the rope, hanging on frantically. Forty feet below him, I could see his face working as he struggled to overcome his nerves. Moving along the rope jerkily, he reached the half-way mark. That was the worst part. The rope was inclined to sway. And Jimmy was shaking – which made it all the worse for him. He stopped. He could take no more. His face was white and damp with sweat. It seemed to be only a matter of time before he would let go and plunge down forty feet to the ground. Bissell was reaching out, trying to steady the rope. And he was still talking calmly. Telling Jimmy to take a deep breath and flex his muscles. Telling him not to look down. Telling him to relax.

'Now – go on,' he snapped abruptly.

Miraculously, Jimmy went on. Slowly and shakily he clawed his way across the rope to the other tree.

Bissell's shout of: 'Okay, come down that rope,' mingled with an outburst of cheering from the rest of the troop. As Jimmy slid down the rope, his knees half-buckling under him when his feet touched the ground, they swarmed around him, thumping him on the back and shaking his hand. I felt like doing the same. I had witnessed an act of true heroism. Quite obviously, heights had always petrified Jimmy. Yet he had overcome his greatest fear. He'd never be afraid of heights again.

And he could never have found the cure any place but Achnacarry.

The 'Death Ride' was Alick Cowieson's brain-child; the 'Tarzan Course' Frickleton's. Who dreamed up the 36-hour scheme – I never found out. But I wouldn't be surprised if it was Vaughan himself. He was a great one for the 'hills'.

A 36-hour scheme was just what the name implies. 36-hours spent away from the camp, tramping over the bleak Lochaber hills, and sleeping out – regardless of the weather. As an ordeal, a 36-hour scheme varied with the time of year. In the summer, it was an almost pleasant break from the camp routine. In the winter, it was hell.

With my usual luck, my first 36-hour scheme – in a troop led by my guardian devil Alick Cowieson – took place in the winter. It was, of course, raining. It rained continuously throughout the 36 hours.

The troop, with Alick and me at its head, set off in a downpour, with gas capes over our denims and packs. By the time we'd marched a couple of hundred yards down the yellow-stoned path to Loch Arkaig, my cap comforter was sodden. Little streams of water from it slowly trickled down the back of my neck. Ah well, only another 35 hours 50 minutes to go!

The gas cape, while it held out against the rain, was a discomfort too. It was inclined to raise steam from the upper part of the body, so that I felt hot and sticky on the march. The lower part of my denim trousers was soaked through with the waterfall from the edges of the cape. From there, the wetness had spread through my gaiters and socks to my feet.

'Don't get your feet wet, Donald,' my mother had instructed me when I left Paisley to come to Achnacarry. And my letters home reassured her that I never permitted such a thing to happen.

In actual fact, I and the rest of the troop splashed through puddles with what looked like gay abandon. But there was method in our apparent madness. It had been discovered that once your feet were wet, it was better to keep them that way. There was nothing worse than socks drying on feet that were still marching. Our route necessitated the fording of the River Arkaig not once – but twice. On both occasions, we waded through the icy water without a shudder.

Darkness was falling as we took to the hills. The troop was grouped into small sub-sections of about ten men each. Follow-my-leader, they bent their knees and shoulder to the slopes.

The tufty spring in the grass was a help or a hindrance depending on

36

whether the foot was placed at the front of the tuft or the back. With the ball of the foot over it, the knee received assistance from the springiness. Those who were regardless of its help, knew all about it in their leg muscles. The wind rose as we climbed until it reached gale force. The rain had a vicious sting in it – not far from hail. Even through the fatigue of climbing, cold showed in every face.

A halt was called in the shadow of Meall a' Phubuill. Above us towered two peaks on either side of the pass we were to go through. It wasn't going to be any fun up there, exposed to the gale and rain without a scrap of shelter.

If ever a brew of tea was called for, it was now. Small fires began to glimmer all around me. I took note of the cunning of the older campaigners. From their pockets and other reasonably dry hiding places, they had produced enough dry twigs to get their water boiling in no time. Others, new to life without a cookhouse, had to search for wood and twigs in the vicinity. The few pieces they succeeded in finding were miserably damp. We'd probably have to move on before their water was more than tepid. But it was their own fault. They should have known better. They had been lectured by the mighty Moon.

Cigarettes and matches, too. Some produced packets squashed to a wet pulp. The wise men took out tins, sealed with adhesive tape. The latter smoked. The former looked at them enviously – and thoughtfully. They'd never make that mistake again.

A sharp command from Cowieson, and we were off again. Off on what – looking back – I consider my most gruelling experience in all the time I spent at Achnacarry.

The initial slope of the pass over the saddle was strewn with boulders, making it extremely difficult for sub-sections to keep any semblance of unity. Instead of a hill walk, we were leaping and scrambling from one rock to another, or perilously slithering up over rock scree. Buffeted by the wind and rain, slipping and stumbling, often on our knees, clutching at tufts of grass, we fought our way up. Here and there men were beginning to show signs of exhaustion and exposure. I took one man's rifle. Somebody else took his pack. Between us we hauled, pushed, and dragged him along while he shivered and moaned uncontrollably.

On the skyline, the full fury of the gale unleashed itself upon us. Men were lifted from their feet and thrown back yards. We had to turn our faces away from the wind, which whipped the breath out of our lungs.

Wet to the skin and half-frozen, our knees wobbling and our teeth chattering, we battled on. Above the gale could be heard the voice of Alick Mor, shouting, encouraging, and exhorting. In answer to his shouts, we gathered our strength, made one last effort – and were through.

The change of conditions on the other side was nothing short of magical. The rain and wind seemed to pass above us and conditions became more moderate. A stumbling run downhill brought us to a dry-stane dyke, on the leeward of which we sheltered thankfully and enjoyed a cigarette. Then off again to the wood Brian Chiolle where we were to camp for the night. Fires were soon lit, and individual rations pooled in groups. A brew of tea and a stew of meat and potatoes raised the spirits of everyone. I found myself thinking that if the inscrutable Sergeant Moon were capable of pride, he would have been proud of the way his cooking instructions were carried out.

After the fires had been used for cooking, bracken and heather were burned and toasted to provide a warm, soft bed on which to lie. The embers of the fire were spread over the area to be used for sleeping. The hot stones were carefully kept. Placed at the feet, they made ideal hot water bottles. Guard duties were arranged. Then, with the rain gushing down through the leaves and branches of the trees, the troop slept. All mod. cons.? Hardly, but if you're tired enough, you'll sleep anywhere. And we were tired enough.

The awakening was miserable. Sodden with the rain, numb with the cold, faces pale, and eyes sunken. Small fires were shiveringly lit. Tea only, with a piece of cold meat and some chocolate – and we were on our way again. The pace was hard, but welcome. With it came heat to our bodies.

So to the grand finale of the 36-hour scheme. A mock attack upon Arkaig Bridge. The men forming into pre-arranged battle formations, we bore down on Achnacarry. I looked at the men around me. Their faces were haggard, their eyes were cold, their expressions were grim. Had it been more than a mock attack, I would have been sorry for the defending forces.

Silently, we crept through the woods. Suddenly, Alick Mor opened that gap-toothed mouth of his. A blood-curdling, wordless, wild Highland cry rent the air. A clatter of feet, a flash of steel – and we were at the bridge. The mock attack – and the 36-hour scheme – was over.

As we marched up to the Castle – what awaited us in the way of refreshment after our efforts? A cold bath! Even now, it makes me shudder to think of it. Yet there were no pneumonia cases. No one even caught a cold. The following morning, out of the 200-odd men who had spent 36 hours in the most savage of weather out in the open, not a single one reported sick. Wet feet the Commando trainees might have – but never cold feet.

If, as I suspect, Vaughan himself was responsible for the 36-hour scheme, he probably got the idea from an incident that happened in the earliest days of Achnacarry. It was a story the Colonel never tired of telling the Mess, and the Mess never tired of hearing.

Vaughan had just taken over at Achnacarry. The first intake had arrived, but training had not yet begun. By way of security, outgoing phone calls were being tapped at Spean Bridge.

An imaginative young trainee phoned up his girl friend, and proceeded to shoot her a most fanciful line. 'It's absolute murder up here, darling,' he said. 'I've been out in the hills for two whole days with 200 other men – and all we had to eat in that time was one slice of bread and butter. I've only just got back to camp. There are still about 150 blokes lost out in the hills.'

A verbatim account of this piece of fiction was sent to Combined Operations H.Q. in London. The gentlemen therein had given Colonel Vaughan a free hand at Achnacarry, and were a little apprehensive about what the redoubtable Charles might be up to. The phoney phone call was all they needed. General Charles Hayden straightaway put in a call to Achnacarry.

'Charles – what the hell is going on up there?' he demanded angrily. 'What about those 150 men? And what's all this about sending hundreds of chaps into the hills with only a slice of bread and butter?'

Vaughan was understandably puzzled. 'I don't know what you mean, sir,' he replied. 'What men? Did you say – bread and butter?'

'Charles, stop beating about the bush,' continued General Hayden. 'What have you done with those men? What the devil's going on up there?'

'I don't know what you're talking about, sir,' protested Vaughan.

'That's enough, Charles,' snapped General Hayden. 'Come down here at once and explain yourself.' And he rang off abruptly.

By pulling a few strings – at which he had few superiors – Vaughan was able to book a sleeper that night. He reported to Combined Operations H.Q. the next day, where General Hayden told him he'd have to make his explanations to Lord Louis Mountbatten himself.

The fable about the bread and butter and the 150 lost men was unfolded for Vaughan's astonished ears.

'But sir,' he pointed out. 'We haven't even started training!'

Lord Louis roared with laughter. General Hayden roared – with anger. 'Why the devil didn't you explain that over the telephone instead of rushing down here?'

'But you didn't give me the chance, sir,' Vaughan reminded him gently. 'You just said: "Get down at once," and banged down the telephone.'

He paused thoughtfully. 'However, now that I'm here,' he added slyly, 'I might as well have a few days leave.'

Again Lord Louis roared with laughter. Again General Hayden affected to be furious. But Vaughan got his leave.

Vaughan had only just returned to camp from leave when it was reported that we now had a Golden Eaglet.

Two N.C.O. instructors, out on one of the hill marches, had spotted an eagle's nest. They planned to capture an eaglet to present to the zoo of their home town in England

On their day off duty, they set off early, equipped with a climbing rope, rifle and binoculars. By 11 a.m., they were cautiously observing the eyrie. There was no sign of the eagle. The N.C.O. with the rifle moved into a position to cover his pal's approach climb to the nest high up on a craggy outcrop of rock. Up and up, he scaled, intent on his footholds, till there before him was the nest – and one golden eaglet.

With their prize, the two hunters sped down the mountainside to the safety of the glen, keeping a watchful eye open for the eagle. As they gave one last look back, they saw the eagle hovering high above the nest, and swooping over the hillside. On return to camp, they made a wooden cage, and attended to their capture with quiet pride.

Vaughan now grimly inspected the eaglet, and the eaglet stared back haughtily, beady eyes unblinking over curved cruel beak. Its vicious talons grated on the wooden spars of the cage, contrasting with the soft creamy down of its feathers.

Vaughan spoke. 'My God! aren't those things protected up here? What will Lochiel say when he finds out we're pinching his eaglets?'

Next morning the camp was astir with the news that the Golden Eaglet was dead. Something had happened during the night. In its panic, it had broken a leg. In spite of the efforts of the two N.C.O.s to tend to its hurt, it had died. The whole camp was upset, and Vaughan as much as anyone.

Naturally, with so much live ammunition flying about at Commando exercises, there were occasional accidents. A bullet ricocheted through a window of Glenfintaig House on the other side of Loch Lochy, directly opposite our boating station at Bunarkaig.

A letter of apology was sent. To follow it, Alick Cowieson was also sent. It goes without saying that Alick accepted the role of ambassador as he accepted everything else – with enthusiasm. If he was going to be an ambassador, he would do it in the time-honoured style. He would *sail* to Glenfintaig House. With a crew of one. Me.

At Bunarkaig, the boating sergeant had a whaler already rigged for us. These huge boats were normally used to train crews in oarsmanship. Manned by twelve or fourteen men pulling steadily in unison, they ploughed the Loch as had the Vikings under Haco. Sometimes they were sailed in mock races, skippered by those adept at the game, when the scene was more like Rothesay Bay at the Glasgow Fair. Alick took command, and we sailed happily out of the little haven into the loch. The day was fair, and the wind fresh and favourable. We had no difficulty in reaching the small pier at Glenfintaig House.

Returning after tea, it was quite different. I knew nothing about sailing, and it now seemed that Alick was no expert either. The sails were raised, after a fashion, but we could make no headway. The wind had strengthened, and we were kept hard pressed to the pier. Exasperated, Alick said, 'Right, we'll have to use the oars.' I had one look at the boat and another at the length of the oars. In my first pull, I failed to get the blade out of the water and the weight of oar coming back sent me over the seat into the bottom of the boat. With a whaler, we usually had two men to one oar, or three men to two oars, one man giving a hand to port and starboard. However, by sitting on the opposite side of the boat to that on which the oar rested, I was able to balance it and pull.

It is only a mile or so from Glenfintaig House to Bunarkaig, but it seemed like ten, pulling as we were against a strong cross wind. When we finally arrived back at Bunarkaig, my hands were blistered and my back felt as if it had been broken. Alick, as usual, was undismayed. He might be no yachtsman, but he had done what he set out to do.

We hurried up the path by the River Arkaig to the Castle. We didn't want to miss dinner, for Alick and I were due to harass a Commando troop which would be lying up in the hills at midnight. Vaughan was at dinner. 'What's on tonight?' he asked. Alick told him. 'Look here, I'll come with you,' he said. With forks loaded and poised, mouths open, Alick and I stared at Vaughan. He meant it. The Laird himself – The MacVaughan – was taking to the hills. It was after eleven, and dark, when the three of us took the road to Achnasaul, passing one end of The Dark Mile with our boots scuffing the yellow gravel on the track along Loch Arkaig. It was a fine night. Vaughan was in good humour, telling his stories.

At Achnasaul, we left the road and climbed by the track which leads to Glas Bheinn. Some way up we paused to allow Alick and me to draw on a last cigarette while we looked down on Loch Arkaig, blue, black, and glassy below us.

Somewhere down there was the tree behind which Cameron of Clunes had awaited an enemy, an English officer of Cumberland's army of occupation, after the '45 Rebellion. This officer had made himself so disliked by his brutal and overbearing manner that Cameron of Clunes had determined to kill him. The officer owned a white horse which was easy to recognise. He heard of the plot and arranged for a brother officer to ride his horse. As the unsuspecting officer rode at night along Loch Arkaig, he was shot dead by Clunes who recognised the horse but not the rider.

I was recalled to the present by Alick carefully stubbing out his cigarette. We were all doubly careful about lighted cigarettes and fires since we had been called out one night to deal with a forest and heather fire which was said to have been started by our mortars.

As we neared the appointed spot, we halted every so often while Alick stood quietly, head tossed up listening like a stag scenting the herd. Finally, he stopped and began his preparations. In a few minutes, he was ready, and his charges went off. I triggered off a few rounds of rifle blank.

Almost immediately our fire was answered. Then – 'Phee-ee-ut! Phee-ee-ut!' Somebody was firing live ammunition! Alick and I lay low in the bracken. I turned to see if Vaughan had crouched down behind us.

And shrank back at a horrible sight. The Laird had gone – in his place was something quite different. The being had two great legs. Its shoulders were thrown back, chest swollen, chin well in, and arms rigidly in line with the seams of the trousers. The face was contorted into a horrifying shape. Awestruck I looked up at the terrifying sight of a Guards R.S.M. about to issue words of command. No Royal stag had ever bellowed in these hills with the roar that had struck fear into the stout hearts of guardsmen at Caterham. 'Who the bloody 'ell is firing live ammunition at me?' There was a silence like the end of the world. Camerons as well as Commandos were holding their peace. It had been a long time since a Redcoat had shouted in these hills, but those with long memories would be reaching for their claymores. At a pace suspiciously like the double march, Vaughan raced past, arms going, elbows well into his side. With a chuckle, Alick was up and after him. I followed.

In the hill camp, there were explanations and mess tins of tea to soothe Vaughan's feelings. No doubt someone laced his tea with whisky to help the armistice. Had some live ammunition found its way into the blank rounds issued? Had someone, knowing Alick, prepared a special thrill for him, not knowing the Colonel would be there also? Or, had the ghost of Cameron of Clunes returned to have another shot at the Englishman in occupation? I asked Vaughan. 'Ghost or no ghost,' he barked, 'if I catch him – I'll pin his ruddy ears back!'

# 6

THE French were coming to Achnacarry. True to the traditions of the Auld Alliance, they were rallying to a standard being raised in Lochaber. The Commando standard. But it struck me that Colonel Vaughan looked slightly apprehensive when he broke the news that a detachment of two officers and twenty-four other ranks of the French Marine Commando were coming to go through the course. And I could understand why. Vaughan had already had one Frenchman at Achnacarry. I had heard the whole story.

It was an incredible episode. To say that the Frenchman concerned was amazingly eccentric would be an understatement. He had been a Governor of one of the French island possessions in the Pacific, and had sailed into Southampton in a yacht to offer his services to Britain. With him he had brought his attractive girl secretary. He was made a Commander in the Royal Navy, and his secretary a W.R.N.S. officer.

As it was doubtless planned to use him in the Pacific islands, with which he was familiar, he was sent to Achnacarry for a course on jungle training. Vaughan never had a moment's peace all the time he was there. A rakish figure with a Van Dyck beard, he arrived in blue battledress, the pockets of which were bulging with a weird assortment of guns and knives. At the drop of a hat, he would demonstrate his prowess with either type of weapon, regardless of safety precautions. Bullets and blades were soon flying all over the place. Vaughan had visions of his staff being sadly depleted.

The Commander's English was not good. Because of this, there was attached to him as an interpreter a very zealous and proper young Royal Marine officer. The latter never seemed to take into account the fact that the Commander was, in all probability, out of his mind. To him, he was merely a superior officer whose every order had to be obeyed, and whose every whim had to be pandered to. As it was, however, the Commander disliked the young Marine intensely. This dialogue became a regular feature of their relationship:

'Soon I weel be sent to the jongle,' the Commander would say.

'Yes sir,' the young officer would agree.

'And you weel be sent weeth me – no?'

'Yes, sir.'

'Do you know what I weel do weeth you when I get you in the jongle?'

'No, sir.'

'I weel keel you!' the Commander would hiss at him.

And the young officer would leap to attention and in clipped tones reply, 'Very good, sir!'

In front of Achnacarry House were some prize rhododendron bushes of which Lochiel was said to be very proud. Vaughan was talking to the Commander in front of them one day when the Irish Q.M., Captain John Carlos, came along to show him a machete – a sort of butcher's knife used in jungle warfare. The Commander's eyes lit up at the sight of it. Snatching it out of Carlos's hand, he brushed past the Colonel and began to hack his way through Lochiel's beloved rhododendrons with wild cries of delight!

Huge chunks of bush flew in all directions, and the Commander, hacking furiously, disappeared from view. Just as suddenly he reappeared again from the depths of the bush and ecstatically brandished the machete under Vaughan's nose, jabbering lyrically about its excellence as a weapon. While the Colonel kept a wary watch on the knife, out of the corners of his eyes he noted the damage to Lochiel's bush. He shuddered. 'My God,' he muttered, and stumped off leaving the Commander slashing at the empty air.

In due course – and not a moment too soon for Vaughan – the Commander had to report to London for a special mission. He was not the kind of man to slip away quietly. Not Monsieur le Commander. He drove away in a car, and knocked down a man in Fort William. Dashing out from behind the wheel, the Commander lifted the man up bodily, propped him against a wall, and poured whisky down his throat. Finally he stuck the bottle in the poor man's astonished grasp and drove away before the police arrived on the scene.

Mercifully, the man was not badly injured, and nothing more was heard of the matter. Nothing more was heard of the crazy Commander either. Perhaps he is still hacking his way through the jungle of some Pacific island to this day, accompanied by his girl secretary and the stiff-upper-lipped young Marine officer. Perhaps he is still hissing at that anxious young man: 'I am going to keel you.' And perhaps the young officer is still springing to rigid attention and replying: 'Very good, sir!'

I felt sure that the Frenchmen now on the way to Achnacarry would be much different from the Commander. Indeed, I found myself feeling rather sorry for the Premier Batallion Français Marins Commandos, as they were known.

We all thought we'd made sacrifices to serve our country. We'd left our homes, our loved ones, our soft beds. The few weeks' leave we got at home seemed all too short.

But these Frenchmen! They couldn't go home on leave. Many of them were probably unsure whether their homes still existed, or whether they would ever be united with the families they had left in haste and stealth.

We had simply been called up, or had volunteered. All that had been involved was a simple, if tedious train journey to our first camp. But these Frenchmen had probably been through all sorts of adventures before they even got to Britain. Now they had been sent to Achnacarry. It was a far cry from Paris in the spring.

I took the liberty of reminding Colonel Vaughan that the Gentle Lochiel fled to Paris after the '45 Rebellion and ended his days in exile there.

'Did he, Donald?' smiled Vaughan. My study of the historical background of the country in which we were trained was a never-ending source of amusement to him.

'Yes, sir,' I said. 'And he was handsomely entertained there. Wined and dined, and provided with luxurious apartments and fine clothes. And now the French are coming to Achnacarry. Strange, isn't it, sir?'

Vaughan looked out of the window at the bleak hills and the eternal rain. He chuckled. 'My God, Donald,' he said. 'Lockiel had the best of it!'

The Premier Batallion Français Marins Commandos undoubtedly shared his view when they arrived at the rain-lashed Spean Bridge station. As a member of the welcoming committee of instructors, it struck me that there can be no more melancholy sight in the world than a group of lugubrious Frenchmen. They huddled together on the platform, misery written all over their expressive Gallic faces, shoulders hunched, chins tucked down into their collars. These were the men who had

46

listened to the strokes of Big Ben – the symbol of freedom – as they were preparing to run the gauntlet of the escape route to Britain. Now another Big Ben was glowering down at them – big Ben Nevis!

A dark, burly Frenchman stepped out from their midst and ceremoniously surveyed the scenery. The others murmured encouragingly, calling him Lofi. He was obviously the wit of the company. His comrades waited expectantly for his pronouncement. It came.

'*C'est formidable,*' he said, lifting his hands in supplication. '*Nous retournerons maintenant à Londres!*'

The laughter which greeted this died abruptly when they learned they had to march seven miles to the Castle. As they formed up ready to move off, they looked glumly at the spate of rain water running down the road.

One of the two officers, tall, bespectacled Leo Hulot tried to console his men with a little humour. 'Nevaire mind,' he called out. 'They 'ave gone to get the boats!'

Then a hush descended on the column. I had no need to look round for the reason. I could hear it. The Pipe Major was inflating his bagpipes.

The French gaped at the performance, and craned their necks to get a better view of the tall, lanky figure of Pipe Major MacLauchlan, his bony knees jutting out beneath his kilt, and one large foot beating time. Whether or not they appreciated the music, I don't know. They certainly couldn't march in time to the pipes. Indeed, the Pipe Major had to be respectfully requested to stop playing before we could get them into step. But throughout their stay at Achnacarry, the bagpipes always fascinated the French. They rarely missed watching the Pipe Band playing 'Retreat'. To them it was "*fantastique*". Maybe it was the show of legs that appealed to them. We had no Folies Bergères at Achnacarry. But we had Pipe Major MacLauchlan and his men!

For our part, we found some of the French customs a little "*fantastique*" too. There was the business of the bread, for example.

Charles Vaughan had anticipated the wants of his new guests as far as he was able. He knew that the French were great ones for eating bread with their meals, and had specially ordered huge quantities. What he had forgotten was that en route to Britain, many of them had perforce been on starvation diets. The bread ritual at meal times was quite fabulous. Orderlies would place large baskets of bread on the tables. Almost as

47

soon as their backs were turned, the baskets were emptied and there was a general uproar for more. This was repeated several times until there simply wasn't any more bread – and the show was over until the next meal time.

Their commanding officer was Captain Charles Trepel, whose happy, round face belied the steel hardness of his eyes. He would fly into spectacular rages to drive his men to the limit of their endurance.

Jean Pinelli was their drill instructor. A noted athlete, his cries of '*A gauche! A gauche!*' mingling with the 'Left! Left!' of the depot drill sergeants gave Achnacarry the romantic atmosphere of a Foreign Legion fort.

Then there was light-hearted Alex Lofi, with a quip for every occasion. I remember once, when I had been thinking along historical lines about these French Marines, it occurred to me that their ancestors might have taken part in William the Conqueror's Commando operation against England in 1066. I challenged Alex about this.

'William was mighty careful not to come North,' I pointed out proudly.

Lofi's eyes sparkled. He scanned the hills and grimaced at the weather – which, naturally, was extremely wet at the time.

'*Mon dieu! Les montagnes* and thees rain!'

He thumped his chest.

'*Pour Guillaume et moi – Londres!*'

Yes, there were characters in the ranks of the Premier Batallion Français Marins Commandos. And for me the most fascinating of all was a lean, twenty-year-old artist called Maurice Chauvet.

For Maurice it had been a crazy war. In 1939 he was called up and served on a cruiser. When France collapsed, his ship was in Algiers. It was called to sea again when the French fleet at Mers-el-Kabir was attacked by the British.

Maurice realised to his horror that he might be called upon to fire on British ships. He declared his objections openly. His words were noted, and a few weeks later he was dismissed from the ship at Toulon. Yet, on being demobilised, he was sent back to Paris with a large body of other sailors – to be greeted by a German military band playing in honour of the heroes of Mers-el-Kebir!

His brother Michel, also in the French Navy, fought against the British at Djibouti and at Diego-Suarez in Madagascar. Yet, when

Michel returned to France, he joined the Resistance and later the 2nd French Armoured Division to fight the Germans!

Maurice decided to escape to England. His escape route took him via Spain where he spent many wretched months in the infamous Spanish concentration camp at Miranda de Ebro. Maurice had been a keen Rover Scout before the war. Starved and ill-treated though he was at Miranda de Ebro, he still had spirit enough – fantastic though it may sound – to found a Rover Scout Troop there, whose members came from the unhappy ranks of the refugees who were continuously passing in and out of the camp.

The troop was active for nearly two years, held regular meetings, debates, and tests adapted to life in a concentration camp. Its member shared their meagre rations with prisoners even less fortunate than themselves. They kept a large Tally Book in which were written the adventures of the eighty odd members, who came from twelve different countries. This incredible book is now in the possession of the British Scout Federation. It was presented to them during the 1947 Jamboree at Moisson in France.

It had taken Maurice 883 days to get from Paris to Greenock, in Scotland.

If, after hearing his story, I needed any further proof of the indomitable courage of Maurice Chauvet – the speed march at Achnacarry supplied it. You can forget my earlier account of the speedmarch that degenerated into a crazy stag party. That was a phoney. The real thing wasn't funny, not funny in the least.

Speed marches were a regular feature of the Achnacarry training. The men were started on a 7-mile march, and worked up to a 14-mile one. 'March' is a misnomer. The distances were covered by a lung-tearing mixture of marching and running – complete with rifle and full equipment.

The time factor had to be considered. Two hours was the allotted span for the 14-mile speed march. In actual fact, very few managed it in that time. It usually took about two hours and five or ten minutes.

When the day came for the French to tackle this test, I was one of the instructors detailed to accompany them. I joined them at the main gate, where a timekeeper stood with a stop watch in his hand. A nod from him, the command 'Quick march,' and the French stepped out. There was always a feeling of tension at the start. The die had been cast, the bridges burned. There could be no turning back or falling out. Every man had to finish the course, even if he had to be carried.

Right from the start, the instructors were hard at work getting the men to march as a team, running up and down the line calling the step and checking on every man. The results of their efforts became evident after a mile of so. The change from quick march to double march was made in perfect unison. The vehicle had been run in, and the gears now changed smoothly.

Boots crashed down on the hard surface of the road in a steady beat for mile after mile. Faces became red. Breathing became laboured. The going was gradually beginning to tell. If equipment had been carelessly fixed or a sock wrinkled when it was pulled on, it would be just too bad. The resultant agonies would have to be suffered.

A mark on the roadside seven miles out indicated the turning point, and the return journey began. As I jogged along at their side, I eyed my French charges anxiously. They were moving like robots, men in a trance, numb. It was cruel. It was inhuman. These men had suffered too much already in getting to Britain to be tortured like this. Two or three of them were obviously in distress. Packs and rifles were silently taken from them by their more robust companions.

Rather to my surprise, I noticed that Maurice Chauvet appeared to be the most seriously affected of all. His face was contorted by pain, he was limping badly, and his eyes were like those of a wounded animal. As the miles went remorselessly by, his condition became truly alarming. His breath came in whines and moans. He was staggering. I spoke words of encouragement to him, but I doubt if he even heard me.

At last we came to the turning at Bunarkaig. The home stretch. Prominently displayed was a notice: 'To Berlin – the Führer is at home.' But nobody laughed. Humour is only a memory when your lungs are on fire, your legs are like rubber bands, and your feet like huge lumps of lead.

Time now for that heart-pounding final effort. A long rise and a quick dip to a stretch of level ground was all that was before us.

'At the double – march!'

The zombies lurched forward, up the rise, then down the hill on legs that weren't quite under control. A bend – and disaster for Maurice. He ran straight off the road and plunged head first over the grass verge and into the ditch. From him there had been no corner. He hadn't seen it. He probably hadn't seen anything for the last four miles.

Two of his comrades grabbed him and hauled him out of the peaty mud. They dragged him on to the road and stood him up between them. Maurice was as near to being unconscious as any man can be without actually passing out. But, God only knows how, he got his feet moving again. Head bobbing, arms waving like a puppet, he staggered on with the rest of the men – past the time-keeper and into the camp.

This was a Commando training test. Having already accomplished the near impossible, they now had to do something extra.

Flopping down on the hillside, they loaded their rifles. At varying distances, small metal plates were set up as targets. All had to be shot down. Steadying their thumping chests as best they could, peering through sweat-blinded eyes, the Frenchmen blazed away until the metal enemies had all been cut down.

As the last plate was sent clanging flat, Maurice Chauvet rolled over on to his back and with trembling fingers slowly took off one of his boots. I went over to him, and turned sick with horror at what I saw. Maurice's foot was a ghastly clotted mass of blood.

The M.O.'s examination wrote the postscript to one of the greatest examples of sheer guts I've ever seen. Maurice Chauvet had done the 14-mile speed march with a carbuncle on his foot...

From that moment on, Chauvet and his comrades were treated with new respect at Achnacarry. They were no longer curiosities, sources of amusement. They were men anyone would be proud to serve with. When they finally marched out of the camp and off to the war, their Cross of Lorraine badges were glinting on the highest honour Achnacarry could bestow – the green Commando berets. No men ever did more to earn them than these colourful, gallant French Marines.

# 7

THE French had come and gone. So had several troops of volunteers from the British Army. And so had one or two of the officers who had been posted to Achnacarry at the same time as myself. But it looked as if I was to go on forever as one of Vaughan's instructors.

It was an interesting job – a fascinating job, in fact. Originally designed for a period of five weeks, the course had now been telescoped into four. It was, consequently, even tougher than ever. The gradual change that came over the trainees during those four weeks was a revelation. A revelation of the amazing stamina and adaptability of the human body. A revelation of the unquenchable spirit of the British soldier.

At the end of the first week, they were dead beat, thoroughly miserable, and ready to give up. At the end of the second week, they were still dead beat, still miserable, but not quite so sure about giving up. At the end of the third, they weren't quite so tired. Far from being miserable, they were beginning to get a kick out of the training. Give up? Not on your ruddy life, chum! By the time the fourth week came along, they were positively revelling in the fact that they were fitter than they'd ever been in their lives before. Incredibly, many of them even went over the assault course or 'Tarzan Course' in their spare time – just for fun!

Yes, it was a rewarding job teaching men like these. But a tremendously hard and demanding one. Reveille was at 6 o'clock in the morning, and training went on until 6 o'clock at night. In addition, instructors were out on schemes with the trainees three nights a week – and no one ever thought of asking Vaughan for overtime! The Colonel did not expect his instructors to take the lead and set an example in everything – he *ordered* them to.

It was by no means merely a matter of shoving a chap off the 'Death Ride'. You had to do it first, and do it well. Even if the troop you were

52

taking out on a speed march was full of crack ex-university distance runners, you had to keep your nose in front and set the pace. The inevitable outcome of this sort of thing was that I was fitter and stronger than I had ever thought possible. But I hadn't joined the Commandos just to build up my muscles. I had joined to get into the war. Achnacarry was a great place, but I wasn't planning on making a career out of it.

What did I do? Honestly and unashamedly, I confess that I did nothing. For a start, I had never actually been officially appointed an instructor. Vaughan hadn't said to me: 'I'm keeping you here for a year as an instructor' – or anything like that. I had merely drifted into the job because he happened to be short of instructors at the time. How, then, could I reasonably approach the Colonel today, when theoretically I might be posted to a Commando Unit tomorrow?

I could, I suppose, have marched in to see Vaughan, explained my impatience to get into action, and indignantly demand to be posted. But if I ever had any ideas along those lines, I had the good sense to shelve them quickly. For one thing, Charles Edward Vaughan was a colonel. For another, he was Vaughan. A young lieutenant does not demand things from a colonel if he wants to stay an officer. And if he wanted to stay alive – he certainly didn't demand things from Vaughan!

Colonel Vaughan had a way of dealing with people who tried to lay down the law to him. People like the Colonel in command of a large detachment of Royal Marines, who came to Achnacarry to go through the course. Vaughan insisted that the Marine officers should be put through the training as a squad. The Marine Colonel demurred. He thought they should be allowed to officer their own men through the course. The idea of his beloved Marines being commanded by officers and N.C.O.s other than his own did not appeal to him.

Vaughan pointed out that the Marine officers weren't sufficiently trained to act as instructors at Achnacarry. But the Colonel was adamant.

In the end, Vaughan lost his patience. 'Look 'ere,' he said finally, 'I'm in command up here. If you don't do as I say, you can start marching back to Spean Bridge – or Glasgow, for that matter.'

The Colonel of the Marines was aghast. 'Charles – you don't really mean that?'

'Oh, but I do,' Vaughan assured him. 'And furthermore – you will go through the course with your officers!'

Vaughan had his way. The Marine Colonel duly went through the course with his officers, cleaning his own equipment, running over the assault course, staying out in the hills – exactly as the ordinary trainees had to do. He had threatened to complain to the Commandant of the Marines about his treatment at Achnacarry. But when the course was over he came to Vaughan.

'Charles,' he said, 'I want to apologise. You were absolutely right, and I was completely wrong. It was a wonderful experience. The course was tough, but I thoroughly enjoyed it. I feel as though I've really earned my green beret.'

If a colonel in the Royal Marines (he's now a general, incidentally) couldn't browbeat Vaughan – what chance had I?

I could, perhaps, have employed a more cunning approach and tried to wangle my way round Vaughan and out of Achnacarry. That would have been less dangerous, but equally fruitless. One would have had not merely to get up very early in the morning to put one over on Colonel Vaughan – one would have had to stay up all night plotting furiously. And even at that, one would have been out-manoeuvred in the most masterly fashion. Vaughan, remember, had once been an R.S.M. in the Guards. As a result, his resourcefulness and craft bordered on the supernatural. A fact which was amply illustrated by the supply and supervision of Achnacarry itself – or the Commando Basic Training Centre, to give it its full title.

Many a brass-hat must have pondered the question – exactly whose 'baby' was Achnacarry? Pondered, then given it up as a hopeless task. Commando Group H.Q. and Combined Operations H.Q. were, of course, directly concerned. But they were several hundred miles away from the Highlands of Scotland.

Geographically, Achnacarry came under North Highland District, which was, in turn, under Scottish Command. But there were the interests of the Royal Marines to be considered, too. And even the Admiralty liked to think it had a finger in the Achnacarry pie.

In the centre of this web of uncertainty, Vaughan squatted like a crafty old spider. Whose 'baby' was Achnacarry? North Highland District, Scottish Command, Commando Group H.Q., Combined Operations H.Q., the Royal Marines, the Admiralty – all might have

Lt.-Colonel CHARLES E. VAUGHAN, O.B.E., Commandant of the Commando Depot at Achnacarry from its formation until 1945 is here seen (left) talking to Brigadier Lord Lovat, D.S.O., M.C., whose name is particularly associated with No. 4 Commando. Colonel Vaughan served in the ranks with the Coldstream Guards throughout the 1914–18 War: he later transferred to the Buffs as Regimental Sergeant-Major and retired in 1935. He was recalled to service in 1940 with the rank of Captain and was in at the beginning of the Commandos. His great achievement was *Castle Commando*, the subject of this book. After the war he became a founder member of the Old Comrades' Association of the Army Commandos. He was a business representative in London. He died in April 1968.

*Spean Bridge Station*

*Achnacarry Castle c1930s*

*Officers' Mess, Achnacarry Castle*

Commando Basic Training Centre - Officers' Mess, Achnacarry 1944

Back Row: Lt. R. Wilkie  Lt. A. J. Milne  Lt. H. J. Keigwin  Lt. W. E. Crowther; Rev. T. R. Colman, R.N.V.R.  Lt. F. Tunstall  Lt. M. Drayton  Lt. D. T. Udy

Middle Row: Capt. J. Balchin  Lt. J. Myers  Lt. R. Parkinson-Cumine  Lt. G. A. Keen, Asst. Adjutant  Capt. T. A. Blandford  Lt. R. Ferguson  Lt. H. C. Blanch

Lt. D. N. Paine  Lt. H. Ellis  2/Lt. W. Nash

Front Row: Capt. K. G. Allen  Capt. J. E. Symondson, R.A.M.C. Medical Officer  Capt. G. A. Kaye  Capt. J. Joy, Adjutant  Maj. A. G. Komrower, DSO, 2 i/c

Lt. Col. C. E. Vaughan, M.B.E., Commandant  Maj. D. J. Cotton Minchin, Chief Instructor  Capt. J. J. Carlos, Quartermaster  Capt. F. E. Benwell

Capt. J. E. Dunning  Capt. R. L. Sharples, Admin. Officer

The 'graves' at the entrance to Achnacarry

*Abseiling down the walls of Achnacarry Castle*

*Fishing from the Arkaig Bridge*

*The Tarzan Course*

*Crossing the toggle bridge under 'enemy' fire*

*The Achnacarry Fleet at Bunarkaig*

*Landing under 'enemy' fire at Loch Lochy*

their own individual notions. But the real answer was – it was Charles Edward Vaughan's!

Had a lesser man held the reins, Achnacarry might well have suffered from an overdose of meddling. The Commando training broth might have been spoiled by too many brass-hat cooks. But the ingenious Vaughan turned the set-up to his own – and Achnacarry's – advantage, by playing off one would-be overseer against the other. It was a magnificent and sustained performance. No diplomat has ever handled so many, so often, and so well. No poker player has ever played so many hands at once and won them all.

To eavesdrop – either unintentionally or otherwise – outside the door of Vaughan's office while he was on the phone to one or other of his multitude of superiors was an education. Suppose, for example, someone at Commando Group H.Q. came on with a suggestion for an addition to the training. Vaughan would hear him out attentively – and in this, at least, he was not acting a part. If anyone, be he ever so humble, had an idea he thought might improve either the conditions or the course at Achnacarry, Vaughan would give him an audience. If he liked the idea, he would adopt it – in most cases tacking on a little refinement of his own. But in the case of the gentleman at Commando Group H.Q., the Colonel was evidently not impressed.

'There's probably a great deal in what you say, sir,' he replied. His tone was respectful, reasonable. The tone of a man whose only wish was to please everyone. 'But you must appreciate my position up here at Acknacarry. Remember, I've got Scottish Command breathing down my neck. I'd give your scheme a trial in a minute – but what would Scottish Command say? They're touchy about things like that, you know. It might be wiser if we scrubbed the whole idea, just to keep the peace... Yes, I thought you'd see it that way, sir. Sorry, but there it is.'

So much for Commando Group H.Q. – until Scottish Command came on with a complaint about something. 'I'm in complete agreement, sir,' Vaughan would say in conciliatory tones. 'I'd put an end to that sort of thing tomorrow – if it were only up to me. But my hands are tied. I've got to answer to Commando Group H.Q. If they tell me to carry out an exercise, and I don't do it – well, they'll want to know the reason why. You see how I'm placed, sir, don't you? What's that, sir? Yes, you could get on to Commando Group H.Q. about it, but, frankly, I wouldn't advise it. There's always the danger that the idea came from Combined Ops. H.Q. – and you don't want Lord Louis on your top, do you... ? My sentiments, exactly, sir... Let sleeping dogs lie.'

Of course, it wasn't always a question of what Vaughan didn't want. Often it was something he did want, but found difficulty in getting. Like Nissen huts. If any of Achnacarry's 'uncles' let him down over delivery of these, he would straightaway get on the phone to someone else.

'Hello, sir. Vaughan here. I need Nissen huts urgently. You know how we're placed up here, sir. We work hard at Acknacarry trying to win the war – and yet that so-and-so says he can't spare me any Nissen huts. Yes, of course I mean him, sir. As I've explained to you before, sir, I don't see why I should have to go to him cap in hand anyway. Oh, I suppose his crowd are entitled to *some* say in the running of Acknacarry, but somehow we always think of your chaps as being in charge of us. We've sort of come to rely on you, sir – and you've never let us down yet. Now, if you could possibly...'

Vaughan got his Nissen huts! He got nearly everything he wanted. Most of all, he got his own way at Achnacarry. Miraculously, he did all this without actually offending anyone. Little wonder that he was sometimes respectfully – if colourfully – known by the various nicknames of 'The Rommel of the North', 'The Laird of Achnacarry', 'The Earl of Spean', 'Lord Fort William', and 'The Wolf of Badenoch'.

No, there could be no fiddling of a posting away from Achnacarry with a man like Vaughan in command.

As a last resort, I could always have gone to Vaughan, explained how I felt, and asked him if he would arrange a posting to a Commando for me. For, although he could smell a phoney a mile away, he was at heart a fatherly type with every sympathy for a genuine case of hardship. But to go to Vaughan and tell him I wanted to get away from Achnacarry was something I could never bring myself to do. A request like that would have wounded the Colonel deeply. It might even have made him doubt my sanity. Colonel Vaughan probably conceded that Heaven was a better place than Achnacarry – but not much better. He had fallen in love with the Castle at first sight. And his affection for the place deepened with every day he spent there.

Every time an intake had completed the course, Vaughan gave them a farewell speech in what was called the Big Hut – a huge tin shed like an aircraft hangar which also served as the camp cinema. His closing remarks gave a pretty clear picture of how he felt about Achnacarry.

'When you leave here,' he would say, 'you will go to civvie billets and get a special allowance. Don't imagine you get this for nothing. You will go on raids and operations.'

At this point he always spoke in a hushed voice, hoarse with emotion. 'Some of you,' he went on, 'will be wounded. Perhaps badly. Maybe you will lose a leg, or an arm… I tell you now, you don't have to worry. You will be taken care of.'

He paused – and the trainees silently speculated. What was this? A large sum of money by way of compensation? Some specially generous Commando pension?

Then the colonel would deliver his punchline. 'There will always be a job for you – up here at Acknacarry.'

No, I couldn't very well go to a man who felt like that about the place and tell him I was dying to get away from it. Until such times as my services were more urgently required elsewhere, I was stuck with the speed marches, the 36-hour schemes, and all the other Achnacarry trimmings. And looking back, I'm glad I didn't do anything drastic. For the Commando Basic Training Centre was about to experience the most colourful, exciting, and entertaining episode of its history…

# 8

IT was happening in practically every other corner of the world. Sooner or later, it had to happen at Achnacarry… The Yanks were coming!

When Vaughan was officially informed that 600 men and 29 officers of the U.S. Rangers were to be put through the course, he paid the Armed Forces of the USA a very high compliment indeed. He got scared. Scared that the Rangers would find Achnacarry too easy!

A couple of days before they were due to arrive, he called a special staff conference and broke the news.

'The Rangers,' he went on to explain, 'are the cream of the United States Marine Corps. The best, the toughest men in the American Marines. And the United States Marines, gentlemen, are very tough indeed.'

He looked down at his papers, then up again. 'Gentlemen, we are being done a very great honour. These men are coming here – here to Acknacarry – to go through the training.'

He fingered his tie and raised his eyebrows at us. Nobody said a word. We just waited. A statement of policy was due. It came.

'Gentlemen,' he concluded, 'we must make it hard for them – very hard indeed.'

I marvelled at the man. He sat at his desk sedately. He addressed us formally. It seemed all very proper and official. Yet what he was telling us, in actual fact, was that he intended to make each and every Ranger rue the day he had been born. Already, he was probably hatching diabolical plots to be sprung on our unsuspecting American allies – and secretly gloating over the opportunity. The prestige of Achnacarry must be upheld at all costs. The toughest form of military training ever devised was to be hotted up until it was as hot as hell.

I shuddered as a sudden, horrible thought struck me. If it was going to be hell on earth for the Rangers – my God, what was it going to be like for the instructors!

The night before the Rangers were due to arrive, the Achnacarry officers were invited to a dance in Fort William. In view of the importance of the impending occasion, I expected Vaughan to place a ban on any such festivities. Rather to my surprise, he insisted on everyone attending it, including himself. From the dance, we all drove direct to Spean Bridge railway station, and changed into battledress in the waiting-room, ready for the march to camp when the Yanks' train arrived at 5 a.m.

It was indeed an occasion. Colonel Vaughan himself was going to lead the seven-mile march!

The 600-odd Rangers duly arrived, under their genial leader, Colonel Bill Darby. With Pipe Major MacLauchlan playing as he'd never played before – to his biggest-ever audience – they formed up ready for the march. With Vaughan and Colonel Darby at its head – and flanked by the other Achnacarry instructors – the column set off on the historic march.

It was, of course, raining. The Rangers marched along in silence, chewing gum and rubber-necking the scenery. They looked none too happy about everything. Even the healthy tan seemed to be fading gradually from their faces as the miles went by in the downpour.

I was stationed close enough to Vaughan and Colonel Darby to be able to overhear their conversation.

'Say, Colonel,' queried Darby, after a couple of miles or so, 'do you always make your men walk to the depot this way?'

'My dear chap,' replied Vaughan, 'do you see that hill over there?' He pointed to Ben Nevis.

'Yeah. It looks quite a mountain.'

'Well,' said Vaughan, 'my chaps usually run up that hill and walk the eighteen miles back to camp before lunch.'

Apparently, Vaughan intended to seize every possible opportunity for a spot of propaganda.

Two miles later, Colonel Darby, looking more than somewhat weary, asked plaintively:

'Don't you ever call a halt in the Commandos, Colonel?'

Head back, chest well out, Vaughan was setting a cracking pace. Towards the end of the war, when I returned to Achnacarry as his adjutant, he confided to me that at that particular time he was 'feeling like death'. Nevertheless, he replied proudly, 'We never halt in the

Commandos, Colonel. Not until we get to the bitter end.' Suddenly, he smiled roguishly. 'But between you and me, Colonel Darby, I won't be sorry when we get to the camp. My officers and I...'

I realised what he was going to say a split second before he got the words out. I realised, too, why he had been so keen for us all to go to the dance. It was to be used as a weapon in his 'impress the Rangers' campaign.

'My officers and I were at a dance last night,' he said. 'Quite a do it was, too. Lasted right into the small hours of this morning. As a matter of fact, we barely had time to get from Fort William to the railway station to meet you.'

Colonel Darby gaped at him. 'You mean you didn't get to bed last night at all?' he exclaimed. 'No sleep?'

That was Vaughan's moment. 'Oh, dear me, no,' he said blandly. 'Not a wink.'

It was a pretty dispirited bunch of Rangers who finally trooped through the camp gates. As was the Achnacarry custom, they were halted in front of the mock graves.

One Ranger jerked a thumb at the graves and turned to his buddy. 'Some set-up,' he observed. 'They kill you on the march here – and then bury you at the gates!'

When the men were dismissed, one solid American citizen – evidently the possessor of a solid American thirst – addressed himself to Sergeant Taffy Edwards, a member of the highly efficient band of N.C.O. instructors at Achnacarry.

'Hey sarge, where's the nearest bar?'

Edwards pointed back along the road they had just covered. 'It's down that way,' he said.

'Yeah? Is it far?'

'No, not far,' replied Edwards. 'Only seven miles. It's in Spean Bridge, the place your train arrived at.'

'Holy mackerel!'

Another Yank was getting an eyeful of Achnacarry, not far from where Vaughan was standing chatting to some of the American officers. The Rangers slowly surveyed the Castle, the hills, the beeches, the firs, the rhododendrons, the bracken, the Nissen huts, and the park land.

'Get a loada this dump,' he commented, to no one in particular.

I could see that Vaughan had heard this remark. His head jolted back, and his pale eyes narrowed and hardened. His chin jutted out a few extra inches. The wartime Laird of Achnacarry was most annøyed. His castle – a dump? By God, he'd give these Yankees dump!

And he did.

I couldn't help feeling sorry for the Rangers. They'd come to Achnacarry – as the saying goes – right off the boat. Straight from their huge bases with centrally-heated barrack blocks and hot and cold running water – to damp, muddy tents in a remote part of the Highlands of Scotland. No Juke boxes. No Coca-Cola. No blondes. Truly, a sad situation for a red-blooded son of the United States to find himself in.

Vaughan, however, was quite merciless. It was the custom at Achnacarry to simulate actual battle conditions wherever possible in the training. For instance, harrowing enough though it was, the trainee didn't just slide across Alick Cowieson's famous 'Death Ride'. He did it with live bullets whizzing all around him – fired by marksmen skilled enough to be sure of missing when they wanted to – and with hand grenades being tossed into the river below. The same treatment was applied to trainees crossing the toggle bridge.

For the 'benefit' of the Yanks, Vaughan ordered the rifle fire to be supplemented by several tommy-guns. And hand grenades alone wouldn't do. Vaughan wanted underwater demolition charges. As far as the Rangers were concerned, the order of the day was – bigger and better bangs!

But one of these bangs backfired – with embarrassing consequences for Colonel Vaughan. It happened the very first time the Rangers tackled the toggle bridge and 'Death Ride'. Vaughan had Alick Mor and myself out at 5 a.m. that morning laying 'king-size' demolition charges on the bed of the River Arkaig, right under the 'Death Ride'.

I've already hinted at the kind of man Alick was. Tell him to lay an extra-large demolition charge, and he would do the job in style. I knew that – and Vaughan knew it. Later in the day, when the Rangers had assembled on the side of the river where the 'Death Ride' began, the Colonel appeared on the other side to watch the fun. Not only that. We had another interested spectator – Lochiel himself.

One after another, the Yanks came whizzing across the 'Death

Ride', to the whine of rifle bullets, stutter of tommy-guns, and the muffled roars of hand grenades. A nod from Vaughan, and Alick and I let off the first of our demolitions, just as some hapless Yank was approaching the half-way mark on the rope.

'B-o-o-m!'

The waters of the Arkaig spouted up, cascading all over the Ranger on the rope. A cloud of little pebbles from the bed of the river rose up and peppered him. He arrived on our side of the river, dazed, grazed, and drenched.

Another Yank on the rope.

Another demolition.

'B-o-o-m!'

Another dense spray of water and spattering of pebbles.

Then, grinning that evil, gap-toothed grin of his, Alick unleashed his 'special'. This was a demolition he had insisted on concocting himself, without any help from me.

'B-A-R-O-O-O-O-O-O-O-O-M!'

It was a titanic blast. The whole Arkaig seemed to be hurled upwards. Everyone ducked instinctively. I caught a glimpse of the man on the rope, eyes shut, teeth clenched, curling himself into a ball as he hurtled down towards a solid wall of water and stones.

And then we saw it.

For a moment, it hung in mid-air, yellow scales dripping and gleaming. A fish. A ruddy, great fish. A salmon. But not just an ordinary salmon. A veritable prince, a king among salmon. With a resounding smack it hit the water and, belly up, slowly began to drift away downstream. Dead? Oh yes, it was dead all right. The miracle was that – after an explosion like that caused by Alick's 'special' – it was still in one piece.

Lochiel stared at the fish. He had a right to stare at it. It was *his* fish. For some long moments he stared at it. Then he turned his head quietly towards Vaughan.

But the Colonel was looking fixedly the other way – as he had been doing ever since he had caught a horrified glimpse of the salmon. We were doing the same. Vaughan hadn't seen the fish. We hadn't seen the fish. Nobody had seen the fish… There had been no fish.

The whole affair might have been glossed over – especially as the Chief of the Clan Cameron had been none too happy about his eyesight in recent years – had it not been for a strapping Yank sergeant. The latter's eyes lit up at the sight of the salmon. In a flash, he was wading waist-deep in the river. He grabbed the salmon and bore it triumphantly back to the bank. There he proudly deposited his burden right at Vaughan's feet, with the words:

'That sure is some fish ya got there, Colonel.'

Vaughan's face was working. He fingered his tie, looking for all the world like the late Oliver Hardy of Laurel and Hardy fame. What was meant to be a nonchalant laugh died in his throat.

Puzzled by the general silence, the Yank sergeant repeated, 'Yes sir, that sure is some fish, Goddam it.'

It had to happen eventually. Lochiel looked up from the salmon, caught Vaughan's eye, and held it reproachfully. The Colonel had to say something.

'F-fish!' he spluttered. 'Good God! Never seen anything like this before. We don't have things like this happen at Acknacarry. It's utterly…'

His voice faded as he wilted under Lochiel's steady gaze. A hunted look came over his face.

But he received no help from us.

It wasn't every day that we were treated to the spectacle of an ex-R.S.M., now a colonel in the Commandos, being caught red-handed in the act of poaching – and by the Laird himself!

Nor was this the only embarrassing situation in which Vaughan found himself as a direct result of the American occupation of Achnacarry.

As a token of their goodwill, the Rangers presented Vaughan with a jeep shortly after their arrival. It was the first vehicle of its kind ever seen in Achnacarry. What is more, they also presented him with a driver to go with it. The driver was no less a person that a full-blooded Indian chief, complete with hawk-like nose and expressionless features. It was a gesture after Vaughan's own heart. He was tickled pink, both by the jeep and its driver.

Whether the chief was a Sioux, Blackfeet, or Apache – we never found out. But he was a chief all right. At any rate, he certainly acted like one at the wheel of his jeep. Any other traffic in the vicinity had to get out of his way, or be prepared to bite the dust. Speed was an obsession with him. I've never seen any jeep go so fast as that one did with the chief at the wheel. I don't mean to suggest that the chief was a heap bad driver. Reckless maybe, but not bad. How could he be? He was still alive.

The chief's finest hour came one day when he was taking Vaughan on a tour of the various training sites. Leaning forward from the back seat, Vaughan pointed towards a section of British trainees who were training on a steep hillside, and said: 'Take me up there, will you?'

The chief nodded solemnly. 'Me do that, Colonel.' he said in his deep, rumbling voice.

Vaughan, in his innocence, had assumed that his driver would stop the jeep at the point on the road nearest to the section, thus allowing him to walk up to them.

His Indian chauffeur, however, had different ideas. When he'd got as near to the section as he could by road, he gave a sudden wrench on the steering wheel and sent the jeep racing up the hillside, hurtling and bumping over bracken, heather and rocks. It was a journey which will be long remembered by all those privileged to witness it. Vaughan was sent careering about the back seat of that jeep like a berserk billiard ball – only, unlike a billiard ball, he didn't have the luxury of cushions. Up and down, back and forward, and from side to side his bulky figure bounced and tossed. He couldn't even muster enough breath to yell at his driver, who was hanging on to his steering wheel resolutely, and nonchalantly chewing gum as the jeep roared over the Highland hillside.

Finally, just when it seemed that the chief was going to mow down the members of the section, he swung the jeep round broadside on and jammed on the brakes almost in one movement. The Colonel went flying out of the side of the jeep like a cork out of a bottle, and landed scrabbling on his hands and knees on the heather.

The chief's craggy Indian features were devoid of any expression or emotion – a characteristic of the stoical race to which he belonged. The faces of every man in the section were set just as hard – but for a different reason. One smile, one titter, one twitch of an eyebrow – and they'd had it!

But what Vaughan may have suffered at the hands of the Rangers was nothing to what the Rangers suffered at the hands of Vaughan. He drove those Yanks as he had never driven any trainees before, hounded them without pity, harried them without compassion. With the Commando Depot's honour at stake, Vaughan put the United States Rangers to the test. Their training schedule was nothing short of murderous.

And how did the Yanks meet Vaughan's challenge? The blunt truth is, for about the first ten days of the course, they looked like being the biggest flops in the history of the depot. Oh, they were the cream of the Marine Corps all right. And they were tough. They'd gone through the most rugged training courses the military brains of the U.S.A. could devise.

But they'd never encountered anything remotely resembling the rigours of Achnacarry. Even the ordinary course would almost certainly have staggered them. Vaughan's super-duper special proved a nightmare.

The bruised and bewildered Rangers just couldn't cope. They floundered on the assault course, fell off the toggle bridge in scores, got tangled in the 'Tarzan Course', and failed to make the required time limit on the speed marches. As for their drill...

Achnacarry's R.S.M. was a formidable six-foot six-inch giant of a man called James. When irritated, Mr James had a peculiar habit of ruffling his shoulders. And when he saw the way the Rangers slouched about the parade ground, his shoulder blades nearly flew off his body.

R.S.M. James was the type of man who considered the sight of a smart drill squad in action a thing of infinitely more beauty that the Mona Lisa. The languid, relaxed movements of the Rangers seared his Regimental Sergeant-Major's soul. Often, he would turn his head away from the parade ground in disgust, and mutter bitterly:

'A shower! A norrible shower!'

Which was a pretty fair summing-up of the U.S. Rangers' performance to date. They had milled aimlessly around the Achnacarry course like lost sheep. Now, their bodies battered and their morale at rock bottom – they looked as if they couldn't take much more.

Our initial pity for them was perilously near the point of turning to contempt. So these were the supermen from the States? Why, they were nothing but a bunch of phoneys. They had no guts. They couldn't take it...

Then, round about the tenth day of their course, an amazing thing happened. I've seen some transformations in my time, but never one like this. It was difficult to describe. It was as if each and every Ranger had suddenly stopped, taken stock of the situation, and said to himself: 'Wait a minute – what's going on here, you guys? We're in the U.S. Rangers, remember. So that guy Vaughan wants to play rough, huh? Thinks he can make monkeys out of us? He's gonna take the U.S. Rangers for a ride, is he? That'll be the day! Anything a Limey bum can do a Yank can do better. So come on, you guys. Let's get the lead out. Vaughan asked for it and he's gonna get it. We'll tear his Goddam course into little pieces. Okay, you guys? Let's get with it!'

They got with it, all right. When a Yank sets his mind on a thing, he does it in a big way. The Rangers were no exception. It was unbelievable. Almost overnight, their dazed eyes became bright and eager, the spring and swagger returned to their stride. The Rangers were back in business. They charged over the assault course yelling like maniacs, swarmed over the 'Tarzan Course' like squirrels, pushed and shoved to get at that doggone toggle bridge, and cut loose on the speed marches as if it were a race, with a gorgeous blonde as first prize. Yet another Achnacarry miracle had happened in front of my eyes.

Even Vaughan couldn't fail to be impressed by their new-found spirit, and in the end he mellowed towards them. He could afford to be magnanimous, in any case. Achnacarry's proud name had been preserved. There was no longer any need to prolong the Vaughan-Rangers war.

The armistice was unofficially signed one evening when Vaughan had done me the honour of inviting me to take a twilight stroll round the camp with him. We came across a Yank sergeant, leaning against a fence admiring the Highland hills in the gloaming. At the sight of Vaughan, he came smartly to attention. The Rangers were learning fast, all right.

'At ease, my man,' said Vaughan genially, coming to a stop. 'Lovely hills around here, aren't they?'

'They sure are, Colonel,' agreed the Yank.

'Tell me, sergeant,' continued Vaughan, 'what do you think of the course?'

The Yank pondered. I waited impatiently. I had an idea that this was destined to be a historic moment. And I was right.

At last, the Ranger sergeant spoke. 'Colonel,' he drawled, with mingled conviction and admiration, 'you sure got a mighty tough depot here.'

I could almost see Vaughan swell with pride. He'd rather have had that simple, spontaneous tribute than a citation from the President of the United States!

He smiled. 'Your chaps are doing fine, sergeant, just fine,' he said. 'Good evening, sergeant.'

As we walked on, Vaughan was silent for a while. Then he said, 'You know, Donald, these Rangers aren't shaping so badly after all. A bit slack by our standards, perhaps, but a damn fine body of men just the same. They'll do. All they needed was a couple of weeks up here to knock them into shape.'

God was in Heaven, Vaughan was in one of his more benign moods – all was right with the Rangers' world. Indeed, they might have marched out of Achnacarry without another harsh word being spoken, had it not been for one, solitary wise guy on the night assault landing...

# 9

THE night assault landing was by far the most spectacular of all the Achnacarry training schemes. And like the superb showman that he was, Vaughan kept it up his sleeve until the end of the training programme. It was a performance fit to top any bill. A spellbinding affair in wide screen and glorious techni-colour. A dazzling cross between the Blackpool illuminations and Guy Fawkes night. The night assault landing was as close to battle conditions as Vaughan could get – without actually slaughtering half the trainees. It was vintage Hollywood stuff – stupendous, colossal. Even those members of the Achnacarry staff who were enjoying a hard-earned off-duty spell on the night in question would never dream of missing it. Fort William, the dancing, the drinking, the girls, and the pictures – all such thoughts were brushed aside as they rolled up to watch the greatest free show on earth. With the U.S. Rangers in the starring roles, there would be standing room only.

Briefly, the night assault landing was a terrifyingly realistic reproduction of an amphibious operation carried out under cover of darkness. The trainees were loaded into boats at Bunarkaig, the Commando boat station on Loch Lochy. They then rowed or paddled – depending on the type of boats employed – across the waters of Loch Lochy, and carried out a mock attack against a heavily defended section of the shore of the loch. A mock *attack* – yes. But it would be an insult to Vaughan's thoroughness to say that it was against a mock *defence*. The trainees were confronted by an arsenal of weapons, manned by an army of instructors skilled in the Achnacarry art of shooting to miss – but not by very much. Vaughan, of course, had no time for blank ammunition. The weapons of defence, from the mortars to the rifles, spat out live stuff – and spat it out in vast quantities. Carping about the question of supplies, an Army brass-hat once complained that Vaughan used up more live ammunition on a night assault landing than Montgomery had done at Alamein!

Such was the night assault landing. Fascinating to watch – dangerous to take part in. The attack route was carefully planned and predetermined. Any trainee who deviated from it – either from carelessness or cockiness – was asking for a hole in the head.

And that was only the ordinary night assault landing. For the Yanks, of course, Vaughan had cooked up an extra-special version...

The preparations, consequently, exceeded all previous occasions. They had to, otherwise we would have finished up with a lot of dead Americans on our hands. Orders and maps were issued and studied. Sand models were made of the area to be attacked. Boating and boat drill were practised day and night. Dress rehearsals took place over the ground until everyone was familiar with the routes to and from the objective. The Rangers carried out these preliminaries efficiently, but a trifle impatiently. The bigness of the night assault landing was right after their Yankee hearts. This was more like it, bud... The Rangers were rarin' to go.

Darkness was falling on the big night as the final routine checks were made in huts and tents – personal papers, equipment, ammunition. As the departure time approached, watches were synchronised in an atmosphere of mounting excitement. Then the Yanks formed up outside in the pelting rain, quiet commands were given, and in silent eagerness they moved off. I looked back along the column as it marched through the avenue of beeches by the river. The Rangers were a ghostly sight. Faces and hands had been blackened, and brasses dulled. Each man was pinpointed only by an occasional show of teeth or the whites of their eyes. Already they were soaked to the skin. And it was bitterly cold.

We halted at Bunarkaig Pier where the boats were waiting for us. So was the boating officer, genial, chubby-faced Jimmy Keigwin. His teeth showed whitely in a smile, and I could imagine his eyes disappearing into twinkling slits between layers of fat. The Commandos had an assortment of craft here – L.C.A.s, whalers, dinghies, cutters, and canoes. But these, in Vaughan's estimation, were far too solid and seaworthy for the Rangers. So he had laid on a frail fleet of collapsible, canvas, flat-bottomed Royal Engineer pontoons.

One Ranger peered at them closely. 'Okay, we've seen the tarpaulins,' he announced finally. 'Where's the boats?'

The pontoons offered no protection of any kind. And they would have to be paddled across the choppy waters of Loch Lochy. Smoothly, the Rangers filed aboard. The crews, previously chosen, picked up the paddles. A final check to make sure that the two men who would hold the craft inshore at the landing were in position at the bows – then, paddles dipping in unison, we slipped out into the loch, line astern. The crews knelt in the bilges Indian fashion and bent their backs to their strenuous task. There were no sounds other than the swish of the paddles, and the hiss of the heavy rain on the surface of the loch.

Further out, the formation changed to line abreast and the strange Yankee armada ploughed its way through the murky dark. The crews were sweating, but the others shivered with cold and expectancy.

The faint outline of the shore appeared ahead, a gap in the trees marking the landing point. A hundred pairs of eyes peering anxiously into the blackness, the run-in began. The pontoons surged through the water as the Yank galley slaves redoubled their efforts. The edge of the shore slowly took shape until I could pick out faintly the various prearranged landing places.

'It won't be long now,' muttered a Ranger crouching near me.

'It' came a lot sooner than he imagined. With paralysing suddenness, the shore of the loch seemed to erupt. Machine-guns chattered and spat flame. Tracer bullets curved and whined over and around the pontoons. There were dull smacks and gouts of water in the loch behind us as mortar bombs rained down. Verey lights and parachute flares bathed the whole fantastic scene in a ghastly light. Guttural shouts in German rang out along the shore. Even for the Rangers, I thought, Vaughan was going a bit too far. This wasn't a night assault landing – this was Dante's Inferno.

The time for caution and stealth had passed. We sent the pontoons skimming towards the beach. And a Ranger chose that moment to do a very foolish thing. Possibly to demonstrate his disregard for all the lead flying about, he rose off his knees and squatted nonchalantly on the gun-wale of his pontoon. It was the action of a screwball and a sucker. He had been well warned. We had told him that the bullets came so close that there had been cases of paddles being smashed by them. Maybe he thought we were kidding. In any case, he sat there asking for it. And he got it.

Just as we hit the beach, with hand grenades exploding in the shallows all around us, the Ranger gave a shrill cry of agony and toppled over the side of the pontoon. He had been hit by a bullet in the buttocks. The other Rangers near him hesitated sympathetically. This was serious. One of the guys had been hit. Blood was pouring down his leg. The word was passed from Ranger to Ranger like lightning. Their ranks wavered, and for one awful moment it looked as if the night assault landing was going to come to a dead stop.

At this critical moment, above the din of the mortars, machine guns, and hand grenades, came an even more awesome sound. The sound of Colonel Vaughan's voice raised in anger.

'What the bloody 'ell do you think you're doing here?' he bellowed, stamping furiously on to the beach. 'Get moving! Get on with it! He'll be attended to.'

The crisis was over in a flash. The wounded Yank was lugged away to an ambulance which Vaughan always stationed there – partly for humanitarian reasons, and partly to add to the atmosphere of danger. The rest of the Rangers, with the other instructors and myself howling them on, made a crazy dash from the beach through greasy mud and peat bog – with demolitions spewing up earth and stones all around. All of us had to run the gauntlet of these explosions, sweating, stumbling, slipping and swearing. The smoke and acrid smell could be tasted. My lips were dry. Without a pause, we topped a rise and were attacking over rough ground towards a steep hill.

The opposing fire had stopped. Now the covering fire started. From behind us, the tracers whined overhead and sent probing fingers of light into the hill. Mortar bombs thudded into the slopes, pock-marking them with small craters. Gasping for breath and semi-dazed, the Yanks fell into their positions and lay steaming with sweat in the sodden bracken. But for one squad, there was no rest. The demolition squad who had been selected in advance to finish the job.

As they scrambled up the hillside, the firing stopped and an eerie silence descended on the battlefield. The main body waited, staring up into the blackness, the men's ear-drums still buzzing and ringing. At the top of the hill, the demolition squad worked with practised speed. The charge was laid and the fuse lit. A moment's pause to see that there was no mistake about that lighted cord – then off. Their shadowy forms loomed up from the base of the hill, and they threw themselves down beside their buddies, faced the hill, and waited.

71

The seconds ticked by in silence and suspense. Then, in a night of gigantic explosions came the most gigantic of all. A tremendous blast echoed and re-echoed in and out of the surrounding Highland hills. There was a rumbling like an earthquake and the entire top of the hill reared up into the skyline in a grey cloud of flying earth and stones. The landing had been made, the attack pressed home. Now for the withdrawal...

The covering forces opened up again as we headed for the beach, hell for leather. Streaks of light flashed across the sky. The din was deafening. The colours of the rainbow with the noise of thunder. As we pelted on to the beach, threw ourselves over the gunwales of the pontoons, and grabbed our paddles, the covering fire turned to opposing fire again. The orchestra of weapons reached a crescendo. In the stark light of the flares, I caught a glimpse of the conductor, Vaughan, standing grimly beside the ambulance. They were throwing grenades again. Huge gelignite explosions drowned all commands. It was hell – there's no other description for it.

Even when we were afloat again, and paddling away from the beach like madmen, the tracers clawed at us greedily. And the three-inch mortar bombs were plunging into the loch so close to us that we actually paddled into the spray. But, at last, it was over. Numbly, we realised that there was no more noise. The firing had stopped. We were surrounded by a blessed screen of darkness and silence.

Fatigue was later replaced by a strange sense of exhilaration, after we'd left the boats and were marching back to the castle. The Rangers' thoughts turned once again to the man who'd been wounded. Only, by then, he had become a source of amusement rather than shock and sympathy.

'Where did you say he got it, man?'
'You're kidding?'
'Honest?'
'Well, I'll be doggoned?'
'Can you beat that?'
'Right in the ass!'
'Coulda been worse.'
'Yeah, it coulda been *my* ass!'

The wound had now become a joke to everyone – everyone except Vaughan. The man had disobeyed orders and Vaughan could see nothing funny in that at all. As the Rangers went on to complete the last few days of their course, the incident was forgotten by everyone – everyone except Vaughan. I knew that he could be ruthless, remorseless, and merciless if he felt a situation warranted it. But in this particular case, Vaughan surprised even me with his vehemence.

He was giving the Rangers his famous farewell address in the Big Hut. After a few generalities, he got down to what had been preying on his mind. His huge Yank audience was electrified when he suddenly said in confidential tones: 'Now, I don't want to cause an international incident. What I am going to say to you must remain here, in this hut.'

The Rangers had been respectfully quiet before. Now a positive hush descended on them as Vaughan went on:

'A few nights ago, on the night assault landing, a man was hurt. He had been told to kneel in the assault craft. But what does he do?'

Vaughan's voice became harsh. 'He disobeyed orders. He sits on his backside on the gunwale. And the silly bloody fool gets himself shot just as he deserves.'

His voice became quiet again. 'We are at war, gentlemen. We must expect casualties.'

He paused. 'But not needless casualties like this one,' he went on sternly. 'Men who disobey orders and aren't disciplined can jeopardise the whole force. This man could have been responsible for getting you all killed or maimed for life.'

'How would you like to lose both legs?' he demanded. 'Or both arms? How would you like to lose an eye – because of a silly man like this?'

Glancing slowly round the sea of serious, upturned faces, Vaughan announced. 'That man is here with us today. Gentlemen, that man is no use to you.'

His voice rising almost to a shout, Vaughan pointed dramatically at the culprit. 'There he is! Why don't you take him outside and shoot the bloody fool now before he gets you all killed?'

I've never felt so sorry for any man as I did for that unfortunate Ranger. Following Vaughan's pointing finger, every Yank present turned his head and stared at him speculatively. Whether it was due to this scrutiny, Vaughan's denunciation, or the pain in his buttocks, I don't know – but the man positively writhed in his seat, his face

73

deathly pale. It was cruel, perhaps. But Vaughan had taught the Rangers a lesson, and had done it in such a manner that it was a lesson they would never forget.

That night we had what Vaughan often described wistfully in days to come as 'an 'elluva party'. When the fun in the Officers' Mess was at its height, an American officer – whisky glass in one hand and cigar in the other – challenged Vaughan.

'Colonel, sir, about that "Death Ride" you got here,' he said. 'We got a "Death Ride" back in the States, too, you know.'

This, of course, was untrue. The Yanks did introduce a 'Death Ride' into their training schemes in the U.S.A. later. But they adopted the idea from Alick Cowieson's original at Achnacarry. The Rangers' officer was determined, however, to put one over on Vaughan, and had no time for little niceties like the truth.

'Yeah, we sure got ourselves a "Death Ride" – a real big one,' he went on, stretching out his cigar and whisky glass to indicate something enormous. 'This ride goes over a river, too, a real broad river. And do you know what we got in that river, Colonel?'

Vaughan shook his head.

'Down below in the water,' said the Yank, his eyes widening with simulated awe, 'we got crocodiles. The biggest, hungriest crocodiles you ever saw.'

For a few moments, Vaughan was taken in. For a few moments he was deeply impressed. For a few moments he was at a loss for a reply. Then the ex-R.S.M of the Guards rose to the occasion magnificently.

'My dear chap,' he said, 'you fellows were very lucky. Up here at Acknacarry – we usually have the Lock Ness Monster!'

The following morning, the whole camp turned out to say so-long to a great bunch of guys. To the stirring accompaniment of pipes and drums, the Rangers proudly marched past Vaughan in a typical Achnacarry downpour. The Limey Colonel had thrown everything he'd got at them, and they'd taken it on the chin and kept right on going. Just the same, Achnacarry was a dump they'd never forget...

And they never did. There was a postscript to the story of the Yanks at Achnacarry. A postscript I wasn't able to read until some months after D-Day when I went back to the depot to become Vaughan's adjutant. Vaughan told me about it himself.

Evidently the Rangers had distinguished themselves in action in

Italy. Despite desperate resistance and heavy losses, they'd pressed home a vital attack successfully.

'A damned fine show it was, Donald, according to all reports, a damned fine show,' Vaughan told me. 'Not long afterwards, their C.O., Colonel Darby – you remember Bill Darby, Donald? – was at a conference of high-ranking Allied commanders. Alexander was there, and the American General Mark Clark.

'Bill Darby was congratulated on the success of the Rangers. Then he was asked to give his opinion on what had contributed most to their success' Vaughan went on. 'And do you know what he said, Donald? He said:

"Whatever the Rangers have achieved is due entirely to the training we had at a place in Scotland, called Achnacarry!"'

It was a wonderful gesture on Colonel Darby's part. Obviously, Vaughan found it deeply moving. In fact, I could have sworn that I saw... No, surely not... Not Vaughan. I must have been mistaken. He probably had a cold coming on – or something in his eye...

# 10

THE last day of each course at Achnacarry had an atmosphere that was all its own. A strangely light-hearted, high-spirited atmosphere, rather like end-of-term day at school. To complete the illusion, we had the sports. The inter-troop competition. The Commando Games.

Each event had the distinctive Achnacarry stamp. There were none of the conventional athletic trials such as the 220-yards, the quarter-mile, or the mile. No high jump. No hurdles. And certainly no egg-and-spoon race.

Instead, the various troops competed against one another – and the clock – over the assault course and on speed marches. (Yes, speed marches for fun!) On Loch Lochy, they crewed cumbersome, unwieldy craft and rowed against one another in a Commando-style regatta. Under the judicial and highly critical eye of R.S.M. James, they drilled against one another on the square. It was a contest that began with a morning inspection – marks being awarded to the troop with the most spotless, shining billets – and lasted throughout the entire day. The Commando Games, in short, consisted of training schemes of which – one would have thought – the trainees would, by this time, be sick to the teeth. Yet their enthusiasm had to be seen to be believed.

The highlight was reserved for the cool of the early evening. This was a unique Commando institution known as the 'milling'. The idea, needless to say, had been evolved by Vaughan. And from the spectator appeal point of view, it was second only to the night assault landing.

The milling was a fistic fantasy. The contestants wore gloves. The bouts took place within the confines of a boxing ring. But there any resemblance between the milling and boxing ended. Boxing, indeed! It was more like a contest between the gladiators of Ancient Rome.

Each troop selected ten Commando gladiators, who were matched against gladiators of similar weight from another troop. The teams formed up by kneeling in line alongside their respective corners, red or green. They were distinguished by red or green football jerseys. It was a non-stop affair. A blast from the time-keeper's whistle indicated not only the end of one bout – but the start of the next one. Each bout lasted one minute – if it went the distance.

A minute may not sound much. But take it from me, there was more action in some of those minutes than you find in many championship boxing contests. There was no time for sand dancing or bobbing and weaving. The two contestants hit each other with everything they had. For sixty solid seconds, the punches flew as fast as they could throw them. It was fabulous, furious stuff. After only a minute of it, super-fit men were reduced to a state of complete exhaustion.

The recently departed Yanks had summed up the milling with the words: 'That sure is a mighty tough work-out.'

If for no other reason, the milling was memorable for the fact that it paid some attention to the weather. In bad weather, it was held in the Big Hut. If the weather was fine, it was held in the open air – the ring being erected just outside the Castle.

I much preferred the open-air version. It was a magnificent sight. The entire camp assembled round the ring, talking and laughing happily in little groups. The Pipe Major playing a lively selection. The Castle windows reflecting light as if gazing indulgently down on the scene. And a background that Madison Square Garden might envy – the incomparable hills of Lochaber.

The arena was full. The Commando gladiators were at the ready. Everything was in order for the arrival of the Emperor Vaughan. Suddenly there was a rapped command. A thousand boots crashed to attention. The great man was in our midst. He took his seat on a specially constructed dais, and surveyed the scene like Genghis Khan himself.

Vaughan, of course, was the umpire. Instead of giving the thumbs-up or thumbs-down signals, he had two flags – one red, one green. After each bout, one of these would be raised, in a gesture brooking no argument or dissension, to signify the winner. At his right hand sat the time-keeper, a stop watch in one hand and a whistle in the other. The Colonel's eyes were sparkling. He enjoyed the milling.

After sniffing the air as if savouring the evening, the faint smell of pine, bracken and peat, the thrill of an expectant crowd, he gave a curt nod. The timekeeper blew a piercing blast on his whistle. In a flash, the first two men were in the ring.

Gloves whizzed through the air faster than the eye could follow. Arms going like pistons, they tore into each other like starving tigers. No probing for weaknesses. No feinting. No sizing up. No covering up. No defensive tactics at all. First one head then the other was jolted back by a tremendous blow. Every ounce of strength in their bodies was behind every punch. The crowd roared its encouragement and approval. This was no stumbling, slow-paced preliminary bout. There was no such thing in the milling. It was main event stuff all the way through.

Red's football jersey was abruptly stained an even deeper hue as a terrific left hook from Green landed on his nose. Green pressed home his advantage in a whirl of stamping feet and a welter of blows. Red swayed back against the ropes, but as Green came in for the kill, stopped him in his tracks with a defiant uppercut.

The whistle blew, the green flag shot up, and the next two were in the ring almost simultaneously. It was obvious that neither had ever been in a boxing ring before. But it was equally obvious that both were dead keen to have a go. In their eagerness, they ran smack into each other, toppled to the floor of the ring, and rolled over. In an instant, they were on their feet again and wading into each other furiously. About half-way through, Red wound up his right in the manner of someone about to putt the shot. If ever a punch was telegraphed it was that one. But if Red was a novice at throwing punches, Green was equally unskilled in the art of seeing them coming. Red's right smashed onto the side of his jaw and chopped him to his knees. Green got to his feet again, but he didn't know whether he was at Achnacarry or on the end of Southend Pier. The whistle humanely blew before time.

Another pair in the ring. The next wearer of the green jersey obviously didn't fancy this milling lark one little bit. He had survived four weeks of speed marches and 36-hour schemes. He had gone over the 'Death Ride' and toggle bridge unscathed. So what was the sense on going home on leave to the girl friend with half his teeth missing? This milling was a mug's game. He wasn't going to get his face messed up if he could help it.

With this aim in mind, he backed away rapidly from Red's opening flurry of punches. Red tried again. And again Green discreetly faded out of range. The bout looked like being a flop. The spectators jeered at Green. But that peace-loving type refused to be angered.

Then Red did a very foolish thing. He hit Green a resounding wallop high up on the head. And an incredible, almost frightening transformation took place. An expression of concentrated fury contorted Green's placid features. The mouse became a lion. Jeers turned to cheers as he cut loose like Rocky Marciano. Left, right, left, right, left, right – Green fairly hammered his unfortunate opponent round the ring like a blacksmith working at his forge. And, in the end, victory was his. But even though the whistle blew and the green flag went up, Green kept on hammering away and had to be forcibly parted from his revenge. By then, the next two were in the ring and for some moments there was a free-for-all flurry of arms, legs, bodies, and feet.

As it cleared, and the fresh pair had the ring to themselves, a roar of mingled laughter and appreciation went up from the spectators. Red had a head of hair that almost matched the colour of his jersey.

'Good old Ginge!' came a delighted cry from one of his comrades in the crowd.

Ginge grinned his acknowledgement. He was powerfully built, but on the small side – almost six inches shorter than his opponent. The latter was a huge, gangling, ponderous, dark-haired youth – a real farmer's boy type. Slowly and methodically, he measured the distance between himself and Ginge and brought his arm round in a scythe-like swing. Ginge ducked under it, bobbed his head back up again, grinned at Farmer's Boy, and waggled a reproachful glove as if to say: 'Naughty, naughty!'

The crowd lapped it up. Ginge was evidently widely known as a card, a character, a comedian. And it was just as evident that Ginge thoroughly relished his reputation. He obviously loved being the centre of attraction, and meant to give the fans their money's worth. Tony Galento? Just you watch old Ginge, mates!

He was certainly worth watching. As light on his feet as a cat, as full of tricks as a monkey – he set out to make a complete fool of Farmer's Boy. And he succeeded. It was a pantomime of a boxing match.

Ginge beckoned seductively at Farmer's Boy with his shoulder in the manner of the traditional Hollywood vamp. Farmer's Boy responded with another scythe-like swing which Ginge dodged effortlessly – then yawned nonchalantly in Farmer's Boy's face.

He gestured menacingly and extravagantly with his right. Farmer's Boy covered up. Then Ginge danced in, tapped him impudently on the nose with his left, then danced away again, blowing him a kiss.

Farmer's Boy was getting impatient. He came charging in like a bull. Ginge stepped forward and held up an imperious hand, like a policeman on points duty. Farmer's Boy stopped in his tracks, blinked his bewilderment, and glanced around to see what had happened. Ginge promptly slammed a vicious right home to his jaw.

Then came Ginge's party piece. Dropping both his arms loosely by his sides, he stuck his chin out invitingly. The infuriated Farmer's Boy needed no second bidding and unleashed a tremendous uppercut. Ginge's timing was superb. A split second before Farmer's Boy's glove reached its target, he jerked his head back. Farmer's Boy uppercutted nothing but the empty air. Such was the force of the blow that it almost looked as if he would loop the loop and land flat on his back on the canvas.

The crowd howled its head off. Ginge took time out for a quick blow, then, like the born showman that he was, decided to give them an encore. It turned out to be the worst decision he ever made in his life.

He lowered his arms and stuck his chin out again. And Farmer's Boy obliged by bringing another colossal upper-cut 'right off the floor' – as they say in boxing circles. So far, so good. But somehow or other, things went wrong for Ginge from that point on. Perhaps his concentration flickered for a vital moment. Perhaps Farmer's Boy's glove was moving a little faster this time. Perhaps he was trying to embellish the trick by waiting even longer before jerking his head back out of range. Whatever the reason, when Farmer's Boy's glove came up, Ginge's chin was still in the target area.

'THUD!'

It was the father and mother of all uppercuts – and it landed right on the point of Ginge's jaunty jaw.

As one man, the crowd emitted a long 'Ooooooooch!' of awe.

Ginge's neck muscles must have been phenomenal. That is the only explanation I can find for the fact that his head was not chopped off. What did happen was incredible enough. Ginge's feet rose – there were those in the crowd who swore afterwards they rose as much as a foot – off the canvas. His head was going backwards with such force that it took his body along for the ride – so that the unfortunate Ginge assumed a horizontal position approximately four feet off the floor of the ring. For a moment it looked as if a magician had taken over the stage. Then the law of gravity asserted itself and down he crashed to the canvas.

Farmer's Boy, who looked more than a little surprised at his own success, reaped the harvest of a green flag. Ginge was unaware that he had been beaten. He was unaware that he had been fighting. He was even unaware that he was Ginge. It was, indeed, a full five minutes – I was later informed – before he was aware of anything.

After this, it didn't seem possible that the next bout could be anything but an anticlimax. As it happened, it turned out to be the battle of the night. Possibly even the most epic encounter in the history of the milling.

Green knew a lot about boxing. That was obvious right from the start. He had certainly fought as an amateur, and probably even as a professional. He advanced lithely to the centre of the ring, his left extended in the classic manner, his right thumb flicking his nose. He stood there, left toe turned coyly in, swaying like a cobra. Yes, this fellow had had gloves on before. I mentally christened him the Kid. He looked as if he could have gone the distance with Sugar Ray Robinson.

His opponent, Red, on the other hand, didn't look as if he could have gone the distance with Wee Georgie Wood. Oh, he was big enough, and heavy enough. But he had none of the muscular menace of the Kid. He looked more like a big, flabby puppy. I mentally christened him Red the Punchbag – because I had a feeling that was the role he was destined to play in this contest. If it could be called a contest, that is to say. From where I sat, it looked as if it was going to be murder.

Punchbag seemed disinclined to take the offensive – for which I didn't blame him in the slightest. Impatient to give the other trainees an idea of what a real boxer looked like, the Kid moved forward in a killer crouch. A hush fell on the spectators. I felt like turning my head away.

A split second later, I was glad that I hadn't. Punchbag suddenly and amazingly stepped forward. One flabby-looking arm became a blur. A good solid right crashed against the side of the Kid's head, knocked him off his feet, and deposited him on the canvas on the seat of his pants.

White with humiliation, the Kid sprang to his feet – and Punchbag walloped him again. From somewhere round about his ankles, his right curved in a vicious parabola to explode on the Kid's chin.

The Kid was down again!

Again he scrambled to his feet. This time he was a Kid transformed. White-hot with rage, he threw his boxing textbook out of the window and tore into Punchbag with both arms going like pistons.

But Punchbag was a far, far tougher customer than we'd all given him credit for. He didn't budge an inch. Standing his ground doggedly, he traded blow for blow with the Kid – who, on his part, was in no mood for retreat.

Toe to toe they stood, smashing savagely at each other while the crowd went crazy. Blow after blow squelched into face and body. They were dripping with sweat, and starting to sway unsteadily on their feet – but neither would give an inch. It was fantastic, magnificent. Gradually the blows became feebler. They began to lean against each other. And as the whistle blew, their knees buckled and they collapsed to the canvas together – Punchbag and the Kid – comrades in utter exhaustion. It was unforgettable…

This, although I didn't know it as I slaked the thirst of excitement in the Mess later that night, was to be my last milling. At least, my last for many months.

Early then next morning the Adjutant, Joy, gave me the unnerving message: 'The Colonel wants to see you.'

I searched my brain frantically. What had I been up to lately that Vaughan could have taken exception to? I couldn't recall a thing. Just the same, I mentally rehearsed a few excuses on my way to his office – excuses that would only need a last-minute touch here and there to cover any conceivable situation.

'Donald, I've got some news for you,' was Vaughan's opening remark.

His expression was grim. The expression of a man whose duty compelled him to be the bearer of bad tidings. I wondered, for a moment, which of my near relatives had died.

But it was something much more serious than that.

'Donald,' he went on, 'you'll have to leave Achnacarry… today.'

I fought a battle with my facial muscles to keep from smiling. Achnacarry was a wonderful place, but I'd had about enough of it to be going on with. And I could guess what was coming next.

'You've been posted to a Commando Unit,' Vaughan informed me. 'They're stationed at Troon. No. 4 Commando. Lord Lovat's the new C.O.'

Colonel Vaughan evidently felt it his duty to do something to soften this tragic blow. Endeavouring vainly to introduce a note of envy into his voice, he added: 'You're on a good thing now, Donald, eh? Civvie billets and soft living.'

Civvie billets and soft living … These words kept ringing through my head as I said my farewells and with twenty ex-trainees – now fully fledged Commando soldiers proudly resplendent in their new green berets – caught the train to Glasgow. Civvie billets and soft living… No more 36-hour schemes in Wagnerian weather conditions. No more night assault landings. No more speed marches. No more getting my feet wet. From now on it would be civvie billets and soft living…

I got a civvie billet all right. One had been found for me in Troon. It was the answer to an Achnacarry instructor's prayer – a cosy, clean room, a luxurious soft bed, and a motherly landlady who – not content with serving up huge delicious meals – would produce tea and toast at the drop of a hat.

Soft living?

I had arrived at Troon on a Sunday. On the Monday, together with the men I had brought from Achnacarry, I was inoculated and vaccinated. As was normal after medical treatment of this kind, we expected to get forty-eight hours off duty.

But on Tuesday – on Tuesday I was swimming for dear life in pitch darkness off the shore of Arran.

The exercise was an old Achnacarry friend – the night assault landing – made from Tank Landing Craft. The L.C.T.s, being huge and unwieldy, didn't reach the point of touch-down as quickly as smaller assault craft. In view of what happened, I have no wish to attach the blame to anyone – particularly after all these years. Let's just say there was a misunderstanding. With a clatter of chains, the ramp of the L.C.T. went down like a drawbridge – too early. From sheer habit, we dashed over it as fast as we could go. And instead of wading through the shallows, we found ourselves struggling in the water, out of our depths.

The L.C.T. was still edging forward. Those who could grabbed hold of the edge of the ramp. Others clung on to them. From the craft itself, hands reached out to help until it grounded. The water was still chest-high as the main body swarmed out, carrying us with them on their run through the shallows and across the sand.

A roll call was made on the spot. Two men were missing, Orchin and Alchin. Their bodies were washed ashore later. Orchin had been carrying a Bren gun slung over his neck and shoulders. He'd been unable to get rid of it, and the weight had pulled him down. Alchin had seen the danger and had tried to hold him up.

They were still clasped in each other's arms when we found them. It was tragic – and yet it was inspiring too. After only three days with an operational Commando unit, I'd had demonstrated to me the close ties of friendship, the comradeship, and the team spirit that existed in it. What Alchin had attempted for Orchin, Orchin would readily have attempted for Alchin.

My new C.O., Lord Lovat, had only recently taken over No. 4 Commando. The departing C.O., Colonel Dudley Lister, was still in Troon when I arrived.

Tall, tough, and turbulent, Lister was a character.

All ranks in a Commando received a special allowance to cover the cost of lodgings. The money was the man's, to use as he pleased. As long as he kept himself clean and tidy, and appeared on parade at specified times, the Army was happy. Where he lived was his own business. Depending on the amount of his allowance – which he could supplement with his Army pay or from private means – a man could live in a hotel or a tent.

Colonel Lister was probably the only member of the Commandos who had done both.

It was customary for the Commanding Officer of No. 4 Commando and his senior officers to live in Troon's luxurious Marine Hotel. Lister duly stayed there for a time. A difference of opinion with the management, however, ended in the Colonel's moving out in disgust. Whereupon the management heaved a sigh of relief that an awkward situation appeared to be over.

Their horror can be imagined when, looking out of the lounge windows the next day, they saw that a tent had been pitched between the hotel and the eighteenth fairway of the famous Old Course. They also saw Colonel Lister, stripped to the waist, performing his ablutions with great energy and enjoyment.

This strange cold war lasted for days. Days in which the management of the Marine grew more and more uncomfortable. But Lister seemed to thrive on the situation. He built camp fires, cooked his meals, and did his washing right under the lofty nose of Troon's leading hotel. With typical Commando ingenuity, he even laid coil upon coil of barbed wire round his tent as if expecting a siege. As luck would have it, Glasgow Fair came in the midst of the proceedings. When curious Glasgow holidaymakers began rolling up in scores for a look at the eccentric colonel – the hotel opposition wilted, cracked, and finally surrendered unconditionally.

After receiving a handsome apology, Colonel Lister struck camp and magnanimously moved back in. Peace reigned once more at the dignified Marine.

I was made a section leader in B Troop of No. 4 Commando under Gordon Webb. A fellow Scot and a prominent figure in the Glasgow Fruit Market pre-war, 'Webby' – as he was known to the men – had been on the Lofoten and Boulogne raids. The other section officer was a demolition specialist called McKay. Slimly-built, quietly-spoken, but tremendously respected by the men, the Troop Sergeant-Major, Chataway, was a veteran of the Spanish Civil War.

I'd only had time to get to know a few of the men – my Section Sergeant Watkins from Yorkshire, Patey, Keeley, Hurd – when we were moved to the South of England with Troops A, C and F. It seemed that I had joined No. 4 Commando at the right time. There was a raid in the offing.

In England we carried out special training under the second in command of the unit, Major Derek Mills Roberts. We pored over maps, sand table models, air photographs, and drawings of an unnamed area until we were confident of routes and positions. Exercises were held every day over terrain similar to that which we had studied. Rehearsal after rehearsal took place, but we were never given a hint of the intended place of attack. The very idea that a raid was imminent was discouraged. But everyone knew there was something in the wind. The old hands, of course, warned us against being too optimistic. Many a proposed raid had fizzled out into a disappointing anticlimax. So much depended on the weather, the tides, the phases of the moon, and whether the necessary naval vessels could be spared. As the days went by, we wavered between hope and despair.

Then, quite suddenly, as I was hurrying towards the hotel where the officers were staying, just before lunch time, I saw something that stopped me in my tracks. Three Commando soldiers moved across my line of vision. There was nothing unusual in their appearance or dress, but they were carrying armfuls of something that glittered and shone in the sunshine. Armfuls of British bayonets. Bayonets that had been newly sharpened and burnished. Sheffield steel, guaranteed. This was it.

We were soon on the move again, in trucks this time, with the canvas laced at the back. When a stop was finally made and the canvas drawn back, I could smell the fresh sea air. A fleet of ships lay at anchor in a harbour. We climbed down from our transport, formed up, and filed up the gangway of one of them. It was a former cross-channel steamer, the *Prinz Albert*. In peace it had ferried holidaymakers from England to the Continent. It would ferry us in war. At the davits, instead of lifeboats, there hung assault landing craft.

A few days of waiting – in which boat drill was practised day and night until we could file through the ship and board the landing craft assigned to us without a hitch – then the order to sail. There was still much to be done, ammunition to be issued and grenades to be primed. In the midst of this, the Tannoy summoned everyone to the Mess Deck.

The buzz of conversation died abruptly as Lord Lovat appeared, accompanied by an officer in the uniform of an admiral. I had seen pictures of him. There was no mistaking the face of the man who stood up on a box in our midst. This was no land-locked admiral. As Charles Vaughan had once told me, he was 'an 'elluva chap'. Lord Louis Mountbatten.

For several seconds he considered us silently and intently. Completely hushed, we stared back.

Suddenly, he smiled. The effect was miraculous. Everybody seemed to be smiling back at him happily, confidently, expectantly.

He spoke briefly and to the point. The operation was on. He had wanted to have a look at us. Now that he had seen us, he knew he wouldn't have to worry any more. He was certain we would succeed.

A wave of his hand to our salute and he was gone. The voice of R.S.M. Morris rose above the babel as we were dismissed.

'All right now, get cracking.'

When at last the final preparations had all been made, I went to my bunk to snatch a few hours' sleep.

We sailed. The ship's engines beat a steady rhythm. I lay back, rested my head on the pillow, but sleep wouldn't come. I had a lot to think about.

This was the real thing. Curiously enough, I remembered a placard on the bank window at Renfrew: 'Foreign Business transacted here.' Tomorrow there would be some strange foreign business.

I remembered what Vaughan had said to departing trainees. 'You might get badly wounded. You might lose an arm or a leg. You don't have to worry – there will always be a job for you up here at Acknacarry!'

I grinned and fell asleep.

# 11

ACOMMANDO soldier was only expected to do three things. They were – in order of popularity – to go on leave, to go on raids, and to go on and on training.

On my first leave from No. 4 Commando, I made history by spending a day of it at Achnacarry, voluntarily, without coercion, and of my own free will. Nobody even twisted my arm.

There were new faces in the Officers' Mess. Spud Murphy, Peter Saville, Bill Nash, Ronnie Hardy, 'Timber' Woodcock, and Dickie Hooper.

There were changes, too, in the Castle itself.

I turned on a tap in the washhand basin of my quarters – and gazed in amazement at what came out. Was I imagining things – or was that steam rising?

Colonel Vaughan himself was proudly showing me round. He smiled at the look of wonder on my face.

'Hot water?' I asked in astonishment.

Vaughan placed a fatherly hand on my shoulder. 'Donald,' he said, with all the considerable charm he could introduce into his voice – it suited him – 'we had it laid on specially for you.'

But I'd somehow failed to notice, on my arrival, the biggest change of all in the Castle.

A pink gin invariably plunged Charles Vaughan into reminiscent mood. He had one in his hand in the Mess before lunch when he remarked, 'Donald, did I ever tell you that we had a fire here?'

I almost choked over my drink. I might have known. It was bound to happen. Once before an English soldier had come to Achnacarry – the Duke of Cumberland in 1746, after Culloden. And he had burned the Castle to the ground. Now, here was Vaughan telling me that he had nearly done the same.

The Colonel's head was thrown back. His eyes were half-closed. The signs were unmistakable. He was about to tell the whole story in some detail.

'It happened on the fifth of November, 1943 – by no means an inappropriate date, I think you'll agree, Donald. I had Lord Lovat and Colonel Dunning White staying with me at the Castle.'

'About midnight, there was a banging on my bedroom door, and I heard somebody shouting: "If you don't get out quickly, you'll be burnt alive!"'

'As it was always raining at Acknacarry, I thought somebody was playing a practical joke. But, just in case, I got up and opened the bedroom door. The whole centre of the baronial 'all was a mass of flames.'

'I shook Lovat and Dunning White, and we all got dressed as fast as we could. But by this time the fire had such a hold that we couldn't get through the door of the bedroom. So we opened a window and climbed down a drainpipe.'

'It was pouring with rain, an 'elluva night,' he went on, 'We had no fire appliances of any kind, and flames were shooting through the roof of the Castle.'

'We phoned for the Inverness and Fort William fire brigades. The Inverness one took seven hours to arrive. The one from Fort William managed to get to Acknacarry in three hours. But it was a voluntary service and had only a small trailer pump, which took nearly another hour to get into operation. We turned the first jet of water from it on to Michael Dunning White, who was standing there wearing blue silk pyjamas and a dressing gown like a film star. The force of it bowled him over in the mud.'

'This was one of the few bright moments of the evening,' continued Colonel Vaughan. 'By the time the fire had been put out, the whole centre of the Castle had been gutted, and the roof burnt off completely. The Officers' Mess had gone – there wasn't as much as a bottle of whisky left. To make matters worse, Lockiel arrived in a furious temper.'

'It didn't improve when he caught sight of Lord Lovat. As you know, Lovat is Chief of the Fraser Clan. For a moment, I thought I was going to have another ruddy clan feud on my hands.'

'I don't mind telling you Lockiel got an 'elluva lot of compensation – I don't think he did so badly out of it in the end.'

He sighed. 'But *I'm* still suffering for it, Donald. This whole countryside is full of Camerons as you know. And they're all after my blood. Why when I go down to Spean Bridge post office now, they make me stand in the queue and wait my turn.'

'To add insult to injury, do you know what that clown in North Highland District does, Donald?'

I shook my head.

'He goes,' said Vaughan hoarsely, 'and repairs Lockiel's Castle with a tin roof!'

Even if Achnacarry wasn't included in the itinerary, leave was wonderful. But, obviously, we couldn't go on leave every week. Nor could we go on raids every week. Raids on enemy-held territory had to be carefully planned and timed.

Training was different. You just trained, and trained, and trained. Commando training was a continuous process designed to keep a man at the peak of physical and mental fitness.

You might think that after an exciting 'party' like Dieppe, we would find the return to the training routine dull, monotonous, and boring. The answer to that one is – in the Commandos, there was no hard and fast training routine. You never knew where you would be told to go next, or what you would be expected to do when you got there. But the various exercises all had one thing in common – the element of danger. There's nothing dull or monotonous about danger.

It was the right formula. The brains of the Commandos knew their psychological onions. The more difficult a task, the greater the challenge to his physical strength and endurance, the wider the scope for initiative, ingenuity, and cunning – the more eager a Commando was to do it.

From time to time we may have become a little impatient to have another crack at Jerry. But we were never bored.

There were the initiative tests, for example. Usually devised by the Troop Leader, these consisted of small groups of men being sent out to carry out the most weird and wonderful tasks. One such group was once instructed to bring back the fingerprints of the police chief of a large town some distance away. Don't ask me how – but they got the prints!

A power station at Kilmarnock, in Ayrshire, was thought to be quite impregnable. This notion came to an abrupt end when one of the guards on the gate felt a light tap on his shoulder one day, in broad daylight. He wheeled round to find half-a-dozen Commandos grinning at him from within the power station.

There was the snow mountain warfare course. A large hotel in Braemar had been taken over by the Snow Mountain Warfare School. When I heard we were being sent up there, I decided that the least I could do – in such surroundings – was to wear my kilt. So I sent home to Paisley for it. It was in the MacLachlan tartan, of which red is the predominant colour.

When Robert Dawson, who succeeded Lord Lovat as C.O. of No. 4 Commando, saw me in it, he was moved to exclaim: 'By God, Donald, if we go on a raid – you're not landing within two hundred yards of me with that thing on!'

The snow mountain warfare course lasted six weeks. The Braemar hotel served as a base camp. From there, the various troops left for separate areas in the Cairngorms to a hill camp. There they lived and climbed for five days before returning to the base camp to rest and refit for forty-eight hours, prior to another expedition. The chief instructors at the school were two distinguished mountaineers, before whom even the most expert climbers in the Commandos kept a modest silence. One was Squadron Leader Frank S. Smythe, who had written several books on climbing. The other was Major John Hunt, now Sir John Hunt, one of the conquerors of Everest.

Instead of Army packs, we carried huge rucksacks on our backs while training in the Cairngorms. We learned to march with our backs slightly bent to the slopes. To assist further in keeping our balance, we were instructed to march with our hands in our pockets. It was worthwhile going to Braemar to see the expression on R.S.M. Morris's face when he heard this!

The passing-out test at the snow mountain warfare school was to climb five Cairngorm peaks in one day. I could think of a lot of adjectives to describe a test like that – but boring wouldn't be one of them.

We also received training on tanks. A few elderly tanks were turned over to us so that we could learn their weak spots, and how best to destroy them. We even learned how to drive them – after a fashion. To see those tanks careering over the countryside in the hands of Commandos whose enthusiasm outmatched their ability was like something out of a funfair. In fact, it was better than the Dodgems.

On one never-to-be-forgotten day, a party of us were taken to Battersea to subject a railway engine to the same study as we had the tanks. How to destroy one, and – our schoolboy dreams had come true! – how to drive one. I'll always remember the expressions on the faces of the men as we swarmed over the footplate like locusts, let off steam, and blew the whistle. Awe, excitement, fascination, joy. Dieppe had been fair enough – but this was really living!

Once a year, a troop leader was allowed to take his troop 'on Commando' – as it was termed. For a fortnight, his troop functioned as a totally independent unit. The troop leader could take them where he pleased, and carry out whatever type of training he thought fit, without any interference from H.Q. He was also given all that he asked for – within reason – in the way of stores, ammunition, and equipment.

My first experience of going on Commando found me in the exalted role of troop leader. In the absence of Pat Porteous, who had won the V.C. at Dieppe, I had taken over D Troop.

On Commando varied from troop to troop – usually according to the individual likes and hobbies of the troop leader. For instance, Robert Dawson was mad on climbing, and C Troop were heading for the mountains of Wales. My former troop leader, Gordon Webb, was taking B Troop on a tour of the Lake District on parachute bicycles.

D Troop had become known as the boating troop. But I was no boating specialist. Come to that, I was no specialist in anything. So I held a conference with Section Leader Knyvet Carr, and Troop Sergeant-Major 'Carl' Carlyle.

Knyvet was a more than useful confederate. If ever there was an eager beaver, it was he. It was his avowed intention to stay in the Army after the war as a Regular. He was a rather trusting soul, too. For certain training schemes, the packs of all were supposed to be weighted with bricks. The cunning ones rigged up their packs with cardboard boxes, and moaned and groaned on the march convincingly. But not Knyvet Carr. He crammed as many bricks as he could into his pack, and stepped it out manfully. The weights he could carry were phenomenal. Though slimly-built and boyish looking, his strength was prodigious. At Achnacarry, Vaughan had infuriated him by calling him 'Nesbit'. In the Commando, we called him 'Muscles'.

Sergeant-Major Carlyle – like all Pat Porteous's N.C.O.s – was gifted with an intelligence far above the N.C.O. normal.

The three of us put our heads together and composed the On Commando overture. We were on Commando at Buxton, Derbyshire, at the time. At 09.30 hours on Monday, the troop paraded in denims, cap comforters, packs and with rifles. Each man had been issued with ten shillings. Their kit bags had already been dumped at the station.

I gave out the orders. 'You will parade at the railway station, Scarborough, at 16.30 hours tomorrow, dressed and equipped as you are now. Each man will, by that time, have arranged a billet for himself. You will be opposed by police and Home Guard en route. They may detain you for an hour or two if you are caught, to prevent you arriving on time. Go now!'

Off they went, forming themselves into groups of two and three as they did so. The Home Guard and police in and around Scarborough had been alerted by their counterparts in the Buxton area. The dress of the Commandos was noticeable enough. They had been given no railway warrants. I had a feeling there would be a story or two to tell by the following afternoon.

Myself, Carlyle, and two other senior N.C.O.s had the task of moving all the kit bags and stores to Scarborough. The trickiest part of the job came when we had to change trains at York. This meant that 60-odd kit bags, heavy weapons, and boxes of ammunition had to be unloaded from one train and reloaded on to another. We commandeered a luggage barrow, formed ourselves into a small chain, and set to.

A soldier stuck his head out of a carriage near the guard's van and gaped at me in astonishment.

'Hey, boys,' he bellowed to his mates, 'come and see this. There's an officer working!'

This strange phenomenon obviously moved him and his friends deeply. They piled out, lent a hand, and the job was done in no time.

At half-past four the following day, the roll was called at Scarborough railway station. Not a single man was missing. The entire troop had paraded promptly. They were clean, and smart. Their eyes were sparkling. They had obviously enjoyed themselves.

As I had anticipated, they had some stories to tell.

One group had gone into a grocer's in a fairly large town to buy some food. The grocer, an enthusiastic Home Guardsman, had recognised them and raised the hue and cry. Police and other keen members of the Home Guard joined in the chase, which culminated in the Commandos being pursued up and down the crowded passages of the local Woolworth's store! They finally managed to duck out of a side door, and didn't stop running until they were well out of town.

Another Commando was determined to prove that he travels the fastest who travels alone. Also, evidently a firm believer in the axiom that the shortest distance between two points is a straight line – he had caught a train to Scarborough. He had, of course, no ticket. But that was a minor detail. He found a compartment full of Servicemen going on leave, and explained the situation to them. Like true, uniformed brethren of the brotherhood of the railway bilkers, they agreed to help him. The plan was an ingenious one. Whenever a ticket inspector was heard approaching, the Commando retired to the nearest lavatory, accompanied by a rating of the Royal Navy.

The ticket inspector was no fool. He rapped on the door of the toilet when he saw that it was engaged. Whereupon, the sailor half-opened the door and thrust his ticket at the inspector – while the Commando was safely hidden behind the door. The lengths to which the sailor went to discourage any closer inspection of the toilet are best left to the imagination! The arrival of the train at Scarborough posed no problems. A railway has walls. To a Commando, walls weren't things that hemmed in – they were things to be climbed. It was dark at the time. And that was that.

By such devious methods D Troop had arrived in Scarborough. Now that they were there – what was I going to do with them?

Knyvet Carr had travelled to Scarborough ahead of us, and had contacted the C.O. of the Home Guard there, Colonel Phil Kitchin. Colonel Kitchin managed the Royal Hotel for Major Laughton, a brother of the famous actor, Charles Laughton. He invited Knyvet and me to the Hotel for a few drinks, and to see if we could cook up between us some sort of exercise in which the Home Guard could pit itself against the Commandos.

This was not, I may say, nearly so one-sided as it sounds. Contrary to popular belief, the Army did not look down its nose at the Home Guard – at least, the Commandos didn't. We had opposed the wily old warriors of the Home Guard before, in various exercises, and had found them pretty tough nuts to crack. Their experience, cunning and local knowledge made a perfect foil for the youth, enthusiasm and fitness of the Commandos. The Scarborough Home Guard would be a particularly tough nut to crack, being a highly organised body.

Under the mellowing influence of a tankard of ale I glanced out of the hotel window. In the old part of Scarborough, down by the waterfront, Scarborough Castle stood high on a grass-covered rocky mound. Secured battlements scowled over a thick wall which surrounded it, to overlook and guard the harbour. The sight of it conjured up romantic pictures of deeds of valour, chivalry, and daring in bygone days. Dreamily, I said to Colonel Kitchin.

'You defend Scarborough Castle – and we'll try to capture it.'

Colonel Kitchin sealed the bargain with unseemly haste. I could see that he thought I'd bitten off more than the Commandos could chew. And frankly, so did I.

The Castle was a formidable fortress. Huge walls, pitted with age, reared up towards battlements which were twenty feet high at the lowest point. The base of the bastion was firmly embedded in rock, which itself created a steep barrier of considerable height. A seaward landing was out of the question. The beach which half-encircled the Castle was mined. A wire fence showed the danger area. One glance at the main gates convinced me that a frontal attack would be fruitless, and merely asking for a shower of bad fruit, rotten eggs, and bags of flour – plus the jeers of the defending veterans.

I held a conference with the entire troop. They obviously shared my misgivings about the venture. In the end, we fell back on the old Commando formula – when in doubt, do something the enemy considers impossible. The plan was this. While Knyvet Carr was leading a diversionary attack on the Castle gates, myself and the main body would scale the walls of the Castle as near the minefield as we dared.

On the agreed night, I crouched beside the wire round the minefield with fifty per cent of the troop and waited. At the prearranged time, Knyvet and the other fifty per cent launched their mock attack on the Castle gates, complete with thunderflashes, bakelite grenades, and rifle blanks. They made such a din that I later learned that the good people of Scarborough were convinced that there was an air raid on!

Taking advantage of this, we raced towards the rock base of the Castle walls. I thought I was fit and fast. But by the time I reached the rocks, a Commando soldier had not only climbed them – he was right at the top of the Castle walls. His name, appropriately enough, was Tudor, and he lowered a rope of previously collected and interlaced toggle ropes. Tudor had obviously been to Achnacarry.

94

We swarmed up the rope, one after another. There was no opposition. The defenders were all at the main gate repelling Knyvet and his men. Who could blame them for thinking the Castle walls were impossible to scale?

As previously arranged, we mingled unobtrusively with the men of the Home Guard, controlling our chuckles with a great effort. Finally, one of the men could stand the suspense no longer. He tapped a Home Guardsman lightly on the shoulder. The latter turned to look straight into a blackened face under a cap comforter. And a pained voice inquired:

''Ow long are you going to keep us 'anging about, mate?'

The Scarborough Home Guard were the best losers I have encountered. They insisted that we should do them the honour of using their transport. While we were driven in grocer's vans, lorries, and even fire engines, they marched back to the Drill Hall. There, a great spread had been laid on – pies, sandwiches, and gallons of beer. It was a heart-warming evening. The lean and hungry young men of the Commandos laughing and joking with the genial old stagers of the Home Guard. Old stories of World War I and young stories of World War II. The kind of night when you almost got the feeling that maybe war wasn't such a bad thing after all, if it could bring men together like this.

The walls of Scarborough Castle were a tough climb. So were the Cairngorms. But the toughest climb the Commandos ever tackled was 'Operation Brandyballs'. Even now, it still makes my blood run cold to think about it.

'Operation Brandyballs' took place not long after Lord Lovat had left No. 4 Commando to take command of No. 1 Special Service Brigade. It took place not long after No. 4 Commando had been reinforced by the arrival of a new officer, Lieutenant David Haig Thomas.

David was a Cambridge rowing blue, an explorer – he had lived with Eskimos in the Arctic – and something of a comedian. While stationed with a previous unit in the Faroes, he had signed his indents 'A. Hitler'. He claimed he got quicker results that way!

Lord Lovat was replaced by Robert Dawson. As I have previously mentioned, Dawson was mad keen on climbing. With Robert now in command of No. 4 Commando, I had a feeling that before long we'd all be hanging on by our fingernails.

Sure enough. We were stationed in the lovely cathedral town of Winchester at that time. Occasionally we held exercises along the

Cornish coast, using Falmouth as our advance base. On one of these trips, Dawson's eye for heights was taken by a stretch of cliffs just south of St Ives.

The cliffs were known locally as 'The Brandys'. Three hundred feet high they rose. Three hundred terrifying feet, pock-marked by overhangs, chimneys, and all the other obstacles that are meat and drink to the mountaineering enthusiast – and a nightmare for anyone else. No one, in living memory, had ever climbed 'The Brandys'. Very probably, no one had even tried. The good Cornish folk had far too much sense. The idea was utterly out of the question. Absolutely impossible. Why, the cliffs were practically undefended, save by the odd coastguard. If the Germans ever did invade England, even Hitler wouldn't be mad enough to pick 'The Brandys' for his beach-head. For centuries the cliffs had stood haughtily aloof from the fingers and toes of man.

Until the advent of Robert Dawson. This reincarnation of General Wolfe decided that No. 4 Commando would climb 'The Brandys'.

It is an elementary principle that, before you can climb anything, you have to get to the foot of it. At 'The Brandys' this could only be done via a landing from the sea. It goes without saying that this, too, was completely out of the question. The sea tirelessly hurled itself against the base of the cliffs with such unrelenting fury that the level of the water rose and fell twelve feet with every breaker. What kind of boat could land in conditions like that? Even if it did, how could the crew disembark? And what about that broken reef of jagged rocks only a little way out? True, there was a ledge at the foot of the cliffs. But it was a narrow ledge. And rounded at the edge. And as smooth as a baby's bottom. How could men get to that ledge? And if they did get to it – how were they going to get onto it? And if they did get on to it – how were they going to climb the cliffs? From start to finish, it simply wasn't feasible.

At least, it wasn't feasible to anyone except Robert Dawson. He had made up his mind. 'The Brandy's were to be the scene of a rough-landing-on-cliff exercise. An exercise to which he gave the picturesque title: 'Operation Brandyballs.'

Dawson tried to get the Navy to take him ashore. They listened to his scheme, smilingly humoured him, and then politely shook their heads. The Cornish fishermen and coastguards did everything but hide their oars and engines to discourage us. In desperation, Dawson turned to the troop I had taken on Commando. D Troop. The boating troop. Now under the command of Pat Porteous once again.

And Pat and his boys came up with an idea. An old Achnacarry idea. We would be taken close to 'The Brandys' in a Tank Landing Craft, then paddle to the base of the cliffs in R.E. canvas pontoons.

The landing? They had that worked out too. Each craft would carry a kedge – or drag anchor. A man seated at the stern would drop it when the pontoon was about twenty feet from the ledge at the foot of the cliffs. As it caught, he would pay out the line while the others paddled to prevent the boat from turning broadside on to the waves.

One man would also be stationed at the bow. His job was to steady the pontoon as well as he could when the ledge was reached. Then, every time the bow rose to a wave, a man would leap off.

Even on paper, it didn't look good.

After the preview, it looked even worse. By a preview, I mean that we scaled 'The Brandys' the easy way – from the top. This we did by a process technically known as 'abseiling'. Ropes were attached to solid objects – or held by groups of men – at the top of the cliffs. The other end was allowed to fall free over the edge. The man about to descend stood with his back to the cliff edge. With his left hand, he wound the rope over his left shoulder and round his left leg to form a sort of bosun's chair. He then walked backwards over the edge of the cliff – ensuring that his feet were flat against the rock face. By pushing outwards with his legs, and at the same time allowing the rope to run through both his hands, he dropped fifteen to twenty feet before swinging into the face of the cliff again. Using his feet as buffers, he pushed himself outwards again and made another drop. This went on until he had reached the foot of 'The Brandys' and – at a given signal – was pulled back up again.

Thus No. 4 Commando inspected 'The Brandys' at close quarters. And what it saw, it didn't like. Oh, the ascent varied from place to place, all right. But only inasmuch as some parts were fearsomely difficult – others were downright suicide.

For some days, we practised off the rocky shores of St Ives. Meantime, word of the operation had filtered through to high places. On the big day, high ranking spectators were expected. Possibly even Winston Churchill. This being the case, a dress rehearsal was thought necessary.

We were driven in lorries from Falmouth to St Ives. There, we boarded a Tank Landing Craft, together with our pontoons. We cruised along the coast, accompanied by a coastguard vessel – which was to patrol offshore in case of accidents.

The L.C.T. nosed in as close to 'The Brandys' as it dared, and the ramp clattered down. The pontoons headed for the cliffs in two waves. My pontoon was in the second.

Such was the swell that it was only possible to see the first line of pontoons when you were on the crest of a wave. In the trough, you could see nothing but water.

As one of the sweating paddlers caustically remarked: 'It's the ruddy *Queen Mary* you want on this lark!'

We drew nearer to the cliffs, and I could see the Commandos who had been stationed there in advance at various points. They were all expert climbers, equipped with ropes to help anyone who got into dire difficulties. It was reassuring to know that they were there.

By now, the first wave was approaching the ledge. They were almost touching when disaster overtook one of the pontoons.

The kedge must have slipped. The pontoon suddenly swung broadside on to the breakers. As if seized by some gigantic, invisible hand, it was dashed against the ledge of rock, overturning and hurling the men into the swirling, foaming waters.

On the cliff, the guardian Commando angels were electrified into action. Ropes were thrown, and strong swimmers dived to the rescue. Nobby Clark, a huge, powerful fellow in Knyvet Carr's section, was perched fully a hundred feet up. Without a second thought he plunged down into the maelstrom at the base of the cliffs. The force of the impact broke his arm. But Nobby still had the courage and guts left to throw his good arm around a struggling Commando and hold him up until both were rescued.

In the midst of all this, frantic signals were shouted for the second wave, and the surviving pontoons of the first, to turn back. We did so. But where launching the pontoons from the L.C.T. had been one thing – sailing them back on to her was quite another. The ramp was a problem. As the sea ebbed, its edge came up. We didn't want to hit it. The only solution was a crazy type of surf riding. We rode in on top of a wave, paddling like madmen to stay there. As we surged up the ramp, we threw ourselves over the gunwales of the pontoon, and dragged it

98

with us into the dark hold of the ship.

Two men in the stricken pontoon had been drowned. The theory was that their clothing had caught on the boat and it had dragged them down with it to the bottom. But we didn't find out about that until later. At the time, another drama was occupying our thoughts. The crew of one pontoon had succeeded in getting on to the ledge before the order came for everyone to turn back. There were about a dozen men stranded there, including one officer, David Haig Thomas.

As luck would have it, they landed at the most inaccessible part of the ledge. Above them the cliff rose sheer, smooth, and perpendicular. It was late afternoon. It was getting dark. The sea was getting wilder every minute. Coastguards and locals alike agreed that rescue was impossible that day. David and his men would have to stay on the ledge all night, exposed to the bitterly cold wind and spray. Any hopes of getting them off would have to be abandoned until tomorrow.

The rest of us returned to Falmouth in the lorries. That night, No. 4 Commando was strangely silent. The thoughts of everyone were with those men shivering it out on the ledge in sodden, frozen denims, at the mercy of the wind and sea. If a gust of wind caught someone off balance – he'd had it. If anyone became too numb to hang on – he'd had it too.

My thoughts were running along these morbid lines when there was a sudden commotion, an uproar of laughing and cheering. I dashed outside. The incredible had happened. David and his men had arrived back in camp! Their brief explanation was that they'd got fed up hanging about the ledge and had climbed the cliffs and come back to camp.

The incredulous question: 'In the dark?' only elicited from the cold, tired, and hungry group the reply: 'Do you see any so-and-so sun?' So we let the matter drop. It wasn't until 'Operation Brandyballs' had been duly carried out the next day that the full implications of what they had accomplished dawned upon us.

When we paraded the following morning, Robert Dawson was accompanied by his predecessor, Lord Lovat. The latter spoke to us. The gist of what he had to say was this:

Despite the tragedy of the day before, 'Operation Brandyballs' would go ahead today as planned. All non-swimmers, poor swimmers, or anyone who didn't feel equal to the hazards attached to the exercise were to take one pace back. Withdrawal would involve no stigma of any kind. In view of the dangerous nature of the scheme, only those fully confident that they could do it were wanted.

As his words died away, a strained atmosphere enveloped the parade. Every Commando stood as if frozen to the spot. No one moved a muscle, blinked an eyelash, or even coughed – in case it might be taken as a sign of withdrawal.

Lovat looked at Robert Dawson. They both smiled. In spite of the offer, this was what they'd both been hoping for – indeed, banking on. Come hell or high water, the men of No. 4 Commando were going to beat 'The Brandys'.

And this time, beat it we did. Once again we boarded the Tank Landing Craft in St Ives harbour. Once again we launched our pontoons off 'The Brandys'. Once again we paddled in towards those cruel, contemptuous cliffs. The figures dotted here and there on the rock face looked tense. More ropes and belts had been prepared for our second attempt. I hoped fervently that we wouldn't need them.

We didn't. This time there were no slip-ups, no order to turn back. As we neared the ledge, the kedge was tossed over the stern of my pontoon. A few moments of suspense, then it caught. Carefully the man at the stern let the rope slip slowly through his hands, while the crew paddled steadily onwards.

Hold it! Our bow was almost touching the ledge. One moment nearly level with the smooth, rounded rock – the next plunging down twelve feet below it. Up again and the first man threw himself at the ledge, swayed for a moment on the edge, then scrambled away to safety as we went down again.

One off!

Up again. Another flying khaki figure. Another moment of nerve-tingling suspense. Another sigh of relief.

Two off!

Time after time the wind, sea, and law of gravity were defied until everyone was on the ledge – except the two men detailed to paddle the pontoon back to our parent ship.

All we had to do now was – climb 'The Brandys'. Climb cliffs that had never been climbed before. And do it carrying weapons.

We did it. I wish I could describe the climbing operation in detail. But I must confess that I saw none of it. My face was pressed close to the rock face, and my eyes were constantly fixed on a point about a yard above me, searching and straining for a glimpse of the slightest finger- or toe-hold. Indeed, the only times my eyes were not thus occupied was when they were shut. It was quite a climb. If all the near things had been laid end to end, our next of kin would have gone grey at the sight.

This being a Commando exercise, there was no rest when we got to the top. Instead, that little bit extra – an attack, with rifle and mortar fire whining and thumping into the moors behind 'The Brandys'.

At last, we could take it easy. I wandered over to where a group of men were peering over the edge of the cliffs. It was at the spot where David Haig Thomas and his men had made their climb the night before.

Some of David's men were in the group. They were easily recognised. Their faces were deathly pale. Their eyes registered extreme awe and horror.

I realised why when I leant down and looked over the edge. Of all the suicidal stretches of 'The Brandys', this was by far the most lethal. For three hundred dizzy feet, a sheer, smooth, unbroken rock face ran down to the ledge at sea level. I surveyed the area with increasing disbelief. There was no conceivable route. No feasible avenue of holds.

In daylight, no sane person would have even contemplated tackling it. Yet David and his men had mastered this rocky monster – in the dark.

Ignorance had truly been bliss. And courage had meant success.

# 12

I N the spring of 1944, No. 4 Commando got a new catch-phrase. The fabulous little man in the beret, General Montgomery, dropped in on the unit one day. After looking us over, he informed us in his typically clipped, confident tones that he considered us 'real, proper chaps, real, proper chaps'. And that rather quaint expression was on the lips of every Commando for weeks afterwards.

Monty's visit was one of the many signs that something big was coming off – the biggest operation, in fact, in the history of war. Britain was one vast barracks for hundreds of thousands of troops. One vast arsenal of weapons and ammunition. One vast garage for the vehicles of war – tanks, jeeps, lorries, armoured cars.

After catching a glimpse of this fantastic mass of men and material, an anonymous American soldier made a chance remark that was destined to become immortal. He scratched his head and observed in awe: 'It's a wonder this Goddam island don't sink!'

Everyone – Servicemen and civilians alike – knew *what* was coming off. They had been arguing the chances of a 'second front' for months. The invasion of Nazi-dominated Europe had to come.

But very few people knew *where*. And still fewer knew *when*.

By this time, I had become the Adjutant of 4 Commando. And even I, in fact, knew very little. But I would have been very dull if I hadn't been able to put two and two together.

First, we were moved to Bexhill-on-Sea. Then the French Commandos arrived to serve in No. 4 Commando under Robert Dawson, who spoke their language like a native. My memories of Achnacarry were revived by meeting again French stalwarts like Maurice Chauvet, Leo Hulot, and Pinelli, whom I had helped to train.

From then on, I lived a Jekyll-and-Hyde existence in my office. I tacked a notice on my door:

'Knock and wait.'

This process gave me time to slip out of sight any documents not intended to be seen by other eyes – and to replace it with some ordinary, run of the Commando mill matter.

A card index system was prepared in secret to ensure that the Unit would always be at full fighting strength. A complete personal record of every man was compiled. A daily check was made on the number of sick or doubtful.

Dawson had been told that No. 4 Commando were to be used – and nothing else. But he and the second in command, Ronald Menday, still had plenty to do in the way of planning and organisation. Meanwhile, the men were put through training which was ingeniously broken up to disguise its special nature.

Then – out of the blue – we were whisked off to a 'concentration camp' near Southampton.

A 'concentration camp' was the ultimate in security. Once inside it, we lost all contact with the outside world. We were sealed off. There was no slipping out at night to the nearest pub. The only time you slipped out of a 'concentration camp' was when you were slipping out into action. Unless, of course, the whole thing was called off at the last minute.

We were given the 'gen'. This was it. No more messing about. The long-awaited second front was about to be opened. D-Day would soon be dawning. The briefing was a model of prepared detail, a revelation of the magnificent intelligence that had been obtained of the area where we were to land.

No. 1 Special Service Brigade, composed of Nos. 3, 4, and 6 Army Commandos and No. 45 Royal Marine Commando, was to attack and capture the town of Ouistreham, then link up with the 6th Airborne Division. The particular job of No. 4 Commando was to destroy a German gun battery. Evidently our success at Dieppe had not passed unnoticed.

The plan of supporting fire had Monty's signature all over it. We would have the guns of a cruiser and two destroyers at our personal call. Gun batteries would also be mounted on Tank Landing Craft. There would be rocket gun ships, and more Tank Landing Craft converted to carry batteries of rocket guns.

Beach groups and beach-head forces were to land immediately before us. Tanks with flails would clear passages through the mine-fields. Other tanks, which threw large explosive charges like depth charges, would help obliterate concrete.

We listened to all this in awe, and wondered if there would be anything left for us to do.

But we certainly weren't allowed to slack in the 'concentration camp'. Ken Wright, Sergeant Sellars, and Brian Mullen of the Intelligence Section conjured up air photos, maps, and models of the coast, town, and gun battery. Both Sellars and Mullen were fine artists, the former lithographic, the latter a painter. Their huge, hand-drawn, coloured maps were so precise and detailed that, by studying them every day, we came to know the countryside as well as people who had been born there.

Ammunition was a problem. To begin with, we would only have what we could carry ashore with us. Reserves would be non-existent for a day or two.

The problem was solved by reintroducing an old friend from the Snow Mountain Warfare School – the rucksack. No matter what weapon a man carried, he had to load into his rucksack – in addition to the ammunition he was already carrying – fifty rounds of .303 and four mortar bombs. Concentrated food and spare clothing was also carefully packed. When full, the weight of the rucksack was considerable. I, for one, found that when I was wearing it and lay down on my back, I was just about as helpless as a beetle. I couldn't get up without first rolling over and getting on my knees.

We were paid another visit by Monty. And he provided us with yet another catchphrase. We all smiled at his imitation of a cocky Scotsman when he told us that D-Day was going to be 'nae bother at a', nae bother at a''.

His order of the day was rather more formal and inspiring. It kept ringing through my head as – amidst mounting tension and excitement – we boarded the *Princess Astrid*, sister ship to the *Prinz Albert*, which had taken us to Dieppe:

He either fears his fate too much,
Or his deserts are small,
That dare not put it to the touch,
To win or lose it all.

The *Astrid* moved out into Southampton Water to become part of the vast armada of ships that had already gathered there. As I looked over the countless warships, troopers, and landing craft, I found myself thinking that Nelson and Drake would have nodded approvingly.

Although the sky was clear and the weather fair, the wind blew at gale force. Even in the shelter of the port, the ships rolled and tossed. What it would be like out in the English Channel didn't bear thinking about.

It was a critical moment. The men were fit. The men were happy. The men were prepared. They wanted to get on with the job. Cancellation at this stage would have the worst possible effect on morale. And I shuddered at the magnitude of the rearrangements required if the operation had to be called off for several days.

We sailed. In tones that tried desperately hard – but failed – to sound matter-of-fact, the momentous news was broken, and the necessary orders given. We steamed out of Southampton Water in convoy. It was dark. When the sun rose again, it would be the dawn of D-Day.

The wind was still too strong for comfort. The plates of the *Astrid* groaned as she lurched and staggered through heavy seas. Occasionally, the screws raced clear as she topped a wave. I wasn't looking forward to the moment when we would have to transfer to the L.C.A.s. Those flat-bottomed little craft had never been intended for rough seas. I fervently hoped I wouldn't be sea-sick.

The armada of liberation ploughed its way relentlessly across the English Channel. 500 warships. 1,000 transports. 3,000 landing craft. And 100,000 men. Men of every Allied nationality. Men who were trying to get a few hours sleep, playing cards, or just lying awake on their bunks – like me – thinking.

I was thinking about our new comrades in No. 4 Commando, the French. This was the moment they'd been dreaming of throughout the years of their gallant exile. Tomorrow, they were going home.

I thought about their M.O., Dr Lion. A few days before, he had insisted on operating on one of his men. The latter, like most of the French, had reached Britain via a series of prison camps. As a souvenir of those days, he had tattooed on his forehead the words 'pas de chance' meaning 'bad luck'. Dr Lion had erased the defeatist phrase.

The man with the tattoo was destined to come through D-Day and all the fighting afterwards unscathed. Dr Lion was killed at 10 o'clock the next day while attending to a wounded man.

I thought about the young French marine, hardly more than a boy, who had moved heaven and earth to get married a few days before we were sent to the 'concentration camp'. His English girl friend was going to have a baby. He applied for leave to get married, but was told that, because of security, that would be impossible.

But the French lad wouldn't take 'No' for an answer. He went straight to Colonel Dawson and stated his case. He explained that he knew he was going to be killed during the operation, and he wanted his child to have a name.

He got his leave, he got married, and he was killed within minutes of arriving at the beach on the morning of D-Day, just as he had predicted.

I thought of Maurice Chauvet, the Rover Scout. Perhaps it had been the thought of this moment that had kept him going through a speed march at Achnacarry with a carbuncle on his foot.

I thought of Phillippe Keiffer of the intense, blue eyes, who now led the French in place of Charles Trepel who had been killed on a raid. Anyone could tell that Phillippe had been to sea. He had that rolling walk.

I wondered about his son and daughter. Would he find them in Paris? He gave no sign of the personal anxiety which he must have felt. He was to find his daughter safe and well. He was too late to greet his son. The lad had been in the Resistance. He was caught and shot just before Phillippe got to Paris.

I thought about the French. And I felt sorry. Sorry for the Germans…

For the record, my D-Day breakfast consisted of ham and eggs – two eggs. It was still dark as we climbed into the L.C.A.s giving the thumbs-up sign to the crew of the *Astrid*. Flashes split the blackness as the guns of the ships all around us played the overture to invasion. Cruisers and destroyers poured shells ashore. Rocket after rocket whooshed towards the beach defences.

I regretted that plate of ham and eggs as the L.C.A.s wallowed awkwardly ashore. We were all clutching little paper bags in case of sickness. Some of them were being hastily pressed into service. I had to fight back the squeamish feeling I always get when I see others being sick and smell the vomit.

We hit the beach in a grey half-light. It was a ghastly shambles of tangled wire, ships, and men. The enemy fire had taken its toll. The ramps went down, and a new kind of wave dashed itself on the beach. A wave of green berets – no steel helmets for the Commandos. Through thigh-high water we raced ashore. Some of the men grabbed the survivors of the beach group by the scruff of their necks and hauled them on to the beach with them. These poor fellows had gone temporarily out of their minds. Their numbers had been decimated. The few that were left had lost all sense of reason. In mad desperation, they had been trying to dig themselves in – in the water.

Machine-gun fire was still heavy. Several Commandos splashed down wounded in the shallows and were dragged ashore by their comrades. Their weapons and ammunition was salvaged, adding to the already heavy burden that the fit men were carrying.

Where were the marked paths through the mine-fields? Where were the flail tanks to clear the way? The beach was evidently paved with good intentions as well as bodies. We were immediately confronted by a barbed wire entanglement, a concrete emplacement spitting bullets at us, and an open field bearing the ominous notice: 'Minen'.

As a few of us struggled over and cut the wire, Knyvet Carr attacked the pill-box with grenades. He was lucky to be only superficially wounded by a German stick grenade thrown in return. But he silenced the pill-box. Good old 'Muscles'!

With Alistair Thorburn I made my way gingerly along the edge of the mine-field, followed by a long line of troops. We paused to collect ourselves, while Colonel Dawson moved forward to reconnoitre.

Then the French troops, who were to lead, began to crawl inland, using sand dunes and hillocks as cover. Dawson arrived back with blood spurting from a head wound. As I went to him, he roared: 'What the hell do you think you're doing? Get these troops moving! Get them going – and fast!'

It was my turn to blow my top. Roaring like a bull, I bore down on the unfortunate French.

'*Allez, allez! Vite, vite!*'

The French gaped at me as if I was a madman. Then they rose as one and – with a stamp of boot and rattle of equipment – began a speed march along the route to the objective. Sacré bleu, this was Achnacarry all over again!

It wasn't until after the war, when I met another ex-Commando in Ayr, that I learned that my beautiful school French had been taken for shouts of 'Allah! Allah!'

The French later turned off to carry out their particular task – an assault on the Casino at Riva Bella, a German strong-point. With a roar of 'Vive la France!' from every throat, they stormed the Casino in a daring bayonet charge and wiped out the defenders.

One by one, the rest of the troops dropped off at pre-arranged positions for the attack on the gun battery.

Then a disappointment. The guns had been moved. But the enemy soldiers remained.

Winkling the Germans out of their shelters and emplacements was no easy task. The whole area abounded in magnificent firing positions. To make matters worse, the enemy let loose an artillery barrage, despite the fact that many of their own men were still in the target area. And to make things still worse, the wireless crew from one of the supporting ships had been knocked out, and we had no way of stopping the shells which had been sent to help us – but were now a menace.

As my batman, a tough Glaswegian called Jock McCall, put it: 'Talk about the bloody Light Brigade!'

But Ouistreham was captured. Our next job was to link up with the remainder of No. 1 Special Service Brigade. They had landed shortly after us, smashed through the German defences, and joined forces with the 6th Airborne Division, who were holding the high ground north of the River Orne. We caught up with them at the village of La Plein.

A foothold had been gained on Europe. The big question now was – could we stay there?

The Brigade had been done the honour of being given the task of holding the extreme left flank of the British Forces. Our own left flank rested on the sea. We were placed under the command of General 'Windy' Gale of the 6th Airborne Division. The Brigade was grouped around Amfreville. We in No. 4 Commando were established at Hauger.

That, briefly, was the overall picture. But, as I pointed out while dealing with the Dieppe raid, when you're in action you have neither the time nor the opportunity to worry about the overall picture. Isolated incidents are the thing that stick in your mind. We tried to pass on to the forward troops, news received at headquarters. Incidents happened quickly. What we needed was a teleprinter. Sergeant Elliott of the orderly room staff had a brainwave. Using a typewriter and a roll of toilet paper he issued stop press bulletins which could be torn off at the perforation in the paper by runners to and from HQ. And in the five desperate days of battle that followed – with the Germans hurling attack after attack at us – there were incidents in plenty.

Incidents like the death of Sergeant Fraser. A softly spoken Highlander from the Lovat Scouts, Fraser had not taken kindly to all the climbing done by the Commandos in training. He had no head for heights. Indeed, only the persuasion of Lord Lovat himself prevented Fraser from leaving the Commandos.

At Hauger, Fraser showed his true quality. During a fierce German attack, he stood in the middle of a cross roads, coolly directing and encouraging his section, in the face of murderous rifle and machine gun fire. It was an incredible exhibition of bravery. But this was something Fraser could understand. This was different from those crazy cliff climbs that made a man dizzy. This was fighting – fighting fit for a Fraser. When he was finally cut down, his section fought like men inspired – as indeed they were – and the only Germans who weren't driven off were the dead and dying.

There was the incident of the white flag that was waved during another Nazi attack. David Style of C Troop stood up to receive the surrender – and was shot by a bullet aimed between the legs of the German who held the white flag. C Troop went mad with rage and routed the perpetrators of this outrage. And the only German whose surrender was accepted was a dead one.

There was the incident of O'Byrne, a wild Irishman in C Troop. A crack sniper, he had teamed up with two other snipers, one from No. 3 Commando, the other from No. 6. The three of them used to go out after Germans as if it was a day on the moors after grouse.

One day they came upon a German post. The Jerries were repairing their defences, but by some strange chance, not one presented a target. The three deadshots speedily concocted a plan. O'Byrne sauntered out into the open and attracted the attention of the Germans by waving his hands, putting his fingers to his nose, and calling them an interesting variety of names. When the Germans leapt for their weapons to deal with the mad Irishman, the two hidden marksmen cut them down with unerring aim. Then the three of them scampered off chuckling like schoolboys.

There was the incident of F Troop and the hot meal. They were in slit trenches in a wood. Because the Germans were addicted to firing anti-aircraft shells which sent shrapnel spattering off the trees and down on to their heads, the ingenious gentlemen of F Troop had covered in the tops of their trenches, leaving only a small space from which to fire. Such was the set-up when they were visited by the Brigade Major, Michael Dunning White.

Major White was distinctly displeased to learn that the troop had not had a hot meal for some considerable time.

'Captain Coulson,' he shouted.

Len Coulsons's head popped up out of his trench. 'Yessir,' he replied, then promptly popped his head down again.

'See that your men have a hot meal at once,' ordered Major White.

Up popped Len's head again. 'Sergeant-Major!' he shouted.

The head of Sergeant-Major Edwards appeared from the bowels of the earth. 'Yessir,' he acknowledged in turn.

'The Brigade Major says the men are to have a hot meal,' commanded Len.

Edward's reply was lost in the scream of a shell and the crash of shrapnel. When the dust cleared, Major White was lying on the ground cursing. He had been hit in the leg. As he was carried off on a stretcher through the troop lines, the Sergeant-Major's voice was raised again.

'Captain Coulson, sir.'

'Yes?'

'*We* don't want a hot meal, sir!'

And there was the unforgettable incident of Patrick O'Donnell from my own home town, Paisley. O'Donnell was in the signals billet one night when it received a direct hit from a German shell.

I was in the signals room with Robert Dawson when it happened. Ken Kennet, a tall, dark sergeant from Eastbourne, was on duty. Suddenly, a tremendous explosion rocked the building. A second or so later, the door burst open and another member of the signals came in. He was covered in dust, with blood on his head and hands. 'The signal billet's been hit,' he panted.

We dashed outside. The building, once a small villa, had been shattered. The R.S.M., Bill Morris, was already on the scene. We all wrenched at tumbled beams and tore aside bricks, in a frantic search. There was no rest until we had made sure that everyone, dead and alive, had been taken out from under the rubble.

Afterwards, I accompanied Dawson to the Medical Post. My eyes were immediately drawn to a table on which O'Donnell lay. One side of his face had been split open. The M.O. had used a clip to hold the skin and flesh together. A big dark-haired chap with a ruddy complexion, O'Donnell was still conscious, although he'd been given morphia.

As I bent over him, he recognised me. I lit a cigarette for him and held

110

it while he puffed weakly. Between draws, he summoned up enough strength to speak. Something was worrying O'Donnell. Colonel Dawson was at the other side of the table. We both leaned forward to catch his feeble whisper.

'Sir, please… make… sure… I… come… back… to… No. 4… Promise… to… get… me… back… to… the boys.'

I nodded and raised my head. Dawson's eyes met mine. He couldn't speak. Neither could I.

This was the kind of team spirit Vaughan had dedicated himself to fostering at Achnacarry. And, by God, he'd succeeded.

After the first five almost sleepless days of constant defence had passed, and I had time to think I found myself thinking about Vaughan. Thinking that he had done a damn sight more towards winning the war than he would probably ever get credit for. Every single thing he'd hammered into the trainees at Achnacarry had been of inestimable value in the heat of battle.

He had blazed live ammunition at the trainees – the Germans weren't using blanks either. He had driven them out on speed march after speed march – and the early stages of the invasion had been one long speed march. He had sent them out on schemes in all kinds of weather – the war didn't stop when it rained. He had taught them to carry on whatever the setbacks – and they had done it. He had given them green berets – and they had worn them with honour.

The initial frenzy of the German troops – frantically trying to live up to Hitler's boast that an invading army would be driven back into the sea – was at last beginning to die out. There could be no doubt about it now. The crisis was past. The Allies were in Europe to stay.

A remorseless journey of liberation was about to begin. A journey that would stretch from the beaches of Normandy to Berlin itself. And whenever the going was toughest, the Commandos would be sent in.

Yes, it was going to be quite a journey. But I had a feeling the Commandos were going to make it. They'd approached it the right way. They'd come via Achnacarry…

# EPILOGUE

C ASTLE COMMANDO' has long since reverted to its rightful tenant, Colonel Donald Hamish Cameron – son of the Lochiel the Commandos knew – has been in occupation of Achnacarry House for nearly fifteen years now.

Colonel Vaughan has gone. The Nissen huts have gone. So has the assault course, the 'Tarzan Course', the toggle bridge, and the 'Death Ride'. The Lochaber Hills no longer echo to the tramp of scores of boots on a speed march, or to the bedlam of a night assault landing.

Even the Commandos have gone. There are no longer any such units in the British Army. But the spirit and comradeship of the Commandos which was fostered in action, is still very much alive today, even fifteen years later. Ex-Commandos still meet together in towns and cities all over Britain, thanks to their Old Comrades Association. Their *News Letter* is sent to many outposts of the world. They will no more forget Achnacarry than an exile of the Cameron Clan.

The Association was, of course, the idea of Colonel Vaughan. As early as 1943 he foresaw the need for the continuance of the bonds of friendship and sense of brotherhood that had been born in the Commandos. He enlisted the aid of a Glasgow business man, Mr Bill Gilmour Smith – whom he met when the latter was on a fishing trip near Achnacarry – and the organisation was duly begun.

Mr Gilmour Smith was also responsible for the building of a Scottish Commando War Memorial.

In many corners of the world, memorials have been raised to commemorate the deeds of the Commandos in some shape or form. A bridge in Italy is named after a Commando Unit which fought an epic battle to defend it. In Holland, where No. 4 Commando landed on the Mole at Flushing in the teeth of enemy guns and underwater obstacles, a monument has been erected showing a soldier crouching like a tiger about to spring. And in the Hall of Remembrance in Westminster, there is a panel in memory of the Commandos.

It was only fitting that Scotland should have a memorial to the Commandos. Scotland – where the Commandos were trained.

And so, on a hill in the heart of the country where they did their training a memorial was raised. A memorial at once striking yet simple. Three gigantic bronze figures of Commando soldiers, in cap comforters and S.V. climbing boots, facing up to the elements. The work of Scott Sutherland of Dundee Art School, whose design was chosen from numerous others in competition.

Is it just another monument – another Glenfinnan – to another lost cause? Is it for the piper to play and lament again 'Lochaber no more'? Or will those who pay the piper call a different tune? So did Vaughan and his Commandos, who refused to be bogged down in history, tradition and ancient Jacobite sentiment.

Scotland the brave! And Commandos would mutter 'you have to be in this climate'. They saw the country as it is. A wild forbidding land of high mountains, deep lochs and turbulent rivers, where nature is often raw. There were no Elstree film studio effects for them. Scotch mist? 'It's raining', they groaned – and went off into the hills.

The only tradition that Vaughan understood was that for which a man would fight – with all he had. Like Sir Ewan, an ancestor of Lochiel, who with his bare hands struggled desperately against an armed English officer at Achdalieu. Sir Ewan killed his opponent by biting through his throat, then later said – that it was the best bite he had had in his lifetime.

With unarmed combat and mountain courses Vaughan revived the heroic spirit of the past, laughed at fantasies, and got on with the job. 'We work hard here at Acknacarry,' he growled. For he knew that here in Lochaber, is opportunity – for adventure, courage and determination, initiative and spirit – which like special service, is never out of date.

Thousands of visitors from all over the world flock to the Commando Memorial every year. Possibly many of them wonder just what the Commandos were, and why a monument to them should be erected in a remote part of the Highlands of Scotland.

I hope that this book will help them to find part of the answer.

For the rest, they must stand where I often stand, with the 'Three Men on the Hill' at Spean. They, like the hills and glens of Lochaber, are silent, but curiously eloquent…

# THE COMMANDO MEMORIAL

Commissioned in 1949 the Commando memorial was designed by Scott Sutherland who trained at the Duncan of Jordonstone College, Dundee. He created one of most enduring memorials in the Highlands: three immense bronze figures in battledress standing on a granite plinth erected high above Spean Bridge. It was unveiled by Her Majesty Queen Elizabeth the Queen Mother in 1952. In spite of the claims of some the figures are not recognisable individuals, they represent every Commando and the essence of many men went into their creation.

Each year hundreds of Commando veterans make the pilgrimage to attend the Service of Remembrance and Wreath Laying held at the Memorial in November. The monument is in the care of the local Council. In 1996 it was suggested that woodland be planted to the north of it but the Council rejected the proposal. The exposed site belonged to the Commandos living and dead and the memorial had been placed there precisely because of its visibility. The monument should remain unscreened forever.

# THE COMMANDO TRAIL

Park at the Clan Cameron Museum, Achnacarry and proceed on foot.

Please note: Achnacarry Castle and grounds are a private residence. The proprietors, the Camerons of Lochiel, have kindly given permission for visitors to enjoy the Commando Trail. Please keep to the road and respect their privacy.

All the lands surrounding Achnacarry were used for Commando training. It is still possible to trace some of the Commando features in a walk around the area.

Start at the Clan Cameron Museum, which during the war was the Post Office. The rock faces above and behind the Museum were used to teach climbing and abseiling techniques both with and without equipment and weapons. Opposite, in the grounds of Achnacarry Castle, nissen huts of varying sizes provided accommodation, cook houses and indoor training facilities. In the shadow of a Douglas fir, a king-sized hut served as a lecture hall, cinema and indoor arena where unarmed combat instruction was given. It was here the all-action one minute boxing bouts, the famous milling, took place. In front of the Castle was the barrack square where the Commandos drilled. The original 'Death slide' and 'Tarzan Courses' were in the trees flanking the River Arkaig. In the surrounding hills and woods the trainees were taught to live rough and survive behind enemy lines.

The guard room stood at the roadside by the present entrance to the Castle. Between it and the Castle were the infamous graves, marked by wooden crosses recording mistakes fatal in war: 'He failed to keep his rifle clean'; 'He showed himself on the skyline'; 'He was too slow to take cover'. They were not genuine but acted as formidable and salutary forewarnings to incoming trainees.

All instructors and staff at the Commando Basic Training Centre at Achnacarry wore a backing of Cameron of Lochiel tartan behind their cap badge during the years 1942 – 45. The Castle was used as the Headquarters and Officers' Mess for the Centre. During the night of 5th November 1943 the roof and part of the main building were badly damaged by fire. It did not prevent its continued use.

Leaving the Castle behind to the right, the training trail continues along the road. Away to the left were the rugged assault courses and field firing ranges. The latter included snap-shooting targets and a house-clearing scenario with pop-up targets.At the road junction at the eastern end of Loch Arkaig turn right to enter the Dark Mile, a place with its own stories stretching back long before the days of World War II Commandos. The stone bridge by the spectacular Cia-aig Falls was frequently used for ambush exercises. Especially in summer, the pool was a favourite spot in which to cool off after a long, hot, sweaty trek back from the Loch Garry country.

The Dark Mile circuit was used for the trainees' first speed march as it provided a nice five mile round-trip from the Centre - an easy jaunt, laden in battle order and moving together as a complete unit - to be completed in less than fifty minutes.

From the houses at Clunes continue to the shores of Loch Lochy where the 'Achnacarry Fleet' was moored alongside the wartime stone boat house. The fleet was a collection of miscellaneous small boats and landing craft used to develop navigational and practical boat handling skills. Landings were carried out on both the eastern and western shores of the loch and were often the prelude to other exercises. The 'Opposed Landing' was enacted on the shores of Loch Lochy between the boat house and the road junction leading back to Achnacarry. It afforded a spectacular baptism of fire for the nascent Commandos. Live ammunition was used and machine guns, mortars, tracers bullets and flares vied with controlled explosions to simulate real battle conditions. Its basis was the military operation carried out by Lord Lovat's No 4 Commando during the Dieppe Raid of 19th August 1942.

It was at the junction leading back to the Museum that the pipes met the incoming Commando trainees as they marched from Spean Bridge to Achnacarry. It was here too that the pipe band took leave of the trained Commandos as, wearing their coveted green berets, they marched back to Spean Bridge and on to active service overseas.

The battles in which the Commandos fought were some of the bloodiest of the War. They were awarded 38 battle honours, 8 Victoria Crosses, 37 Distinguished Service Orders (9 with bars), 162 Military Crosses (13 with bars) and 218 Military Medals.

In 1993 the Commando Association was granted the Freedom of Fort William and Lochaber.

At the Clan Cameron Museum there is a collection of Commando memorabilia and photographs. The Commando Exhibition Centre in the Spean Bridge Hotel has an excellent exhibition and holds many Commando artefacts.